Areté

ISSUE FORTY-THREE
SPRING/SUMMER 2014

Areté

WE THANK NEW COLLEGE, OXFORD, FOR ITS CONTINUING SUPPORT,
WHICH HAS BEEN CRUCIAL SINCE THE FIRST ISSUE.

'The Greeks felt that areté was, above everything else, a power, an ability to do something. Strength and health are the areté of the body; cleverness and insight the areté of the mind.'

Werner Jaeger: *Paideia*

Areté, 8 New College Lane, Oxford, OX1 3BN, England
Phone: 01865 289193 / Fax: 01865 289194
e-mail: craig.raine@new.ox.ac.uk
www.aretemagazine.com
Unsolicited manuscripts should be accompanied by an SAE

Areté magazine is registered as a limited company 03876680
VAT Number 990 6680 78
ISBN: 978-0-9572999-5-5

Areté subscription information: see page 157

ISSUE FORTY-THREE
SPRING/SUMMER 2014

Guy Mathers

Kyrie Eleison

zdravstvujtye, hi Guy! please forgive me writing
i saw your profile and i liked your picture :)
here are my answers to the questionnaire
'Give three words to describe your character?'
i dont know, may be lonely, quiet, kind…
'What are your favourite hobbies?' i like nature
and sun and rain, i love the simple pleasures :)
'What are your goals in life?' ponder the bible
and use my life to spread the word of god
'Explain why you are interested in marriage?'
I wish to find a strong and christian husband
with whom to go by hands for all my life
(establish me in the path of Your commandments)
'If you should ever argue with your husband
How would you settle it?' i try to cook him
something delicious that was not so angry!
i hope u like this photograph i send you
i will be glad if one day u can meet me
PS: can u say ur opinion me?

* * *

dear Guy, i was so happy with your letter.
im glad u also wish that we will marriage.
im glad because i like romantic persons.
in spring my sister marriage with a german,
she also met him on a christian website.
last night a dream has dreamed me all about!
i dream of taking baths and go to sleep
(the purity of mind and of the body)
and I will massage, Guy do u like massage?

* * *

zdravstvuj my darling Guy and god protect you
I was so glad to speak to you on skype
im sorry that u didnt hear me speaking
i think it is a problem with the network
i pray we meet in life not internet
(let me not be confounded in my hope)
the airplane ticket is 800 euros
and also there is visa and insurance.
Yes Guy I will be glad if you will pay this
you have a little house inside my heart
I cant imagine now a life without you.

* * *

I have bad news and now and now Im crying
the manager at once has seen my passpot
and told me that I must have cash to travel
should be not less than 1500 pounds
I do not where I take this huge sum money
but he explained me I should not break law
I strongly want u with me for excitement
I have a shiver I can not calm down
(and I have sinned exceedingly in thought)
love is the happiest and pleasant feeling
that you and only you can wake inside me
to burn eternally inside my body!!!

I wish to have with you a Christian children
but Guy I do not wish to break the law
(deliver me according to your word)
so can u make a transfer western union
I think I saw a bank outside the airpot

* * *

my dear Guy, i dont understand why angry?
i think i didnt make anything wrong
i love you Guy and so i dont wish lost u
i didnt phone because i am on rouming
my love i was at custom and they told me
that i cant leave because i have a dept
(in what I have done and what I have failed to do)
i must pay dept of 40000 rubl
and now i moscow nobody cant help me
and u are angry i dont what to do
i wish that i will be with u forever
but also i will need 600 pounds

* * *

zdravstvujtye, i will back to ur ur money
ok now i will go again to home
when i will be at home i back ur money
(bring us to everlasting life. Amen)
and then i never write to u again

* * *

Dear Mr. Mathers, Thank you for your letter.
In my opinion, in your situation,
a criminal, not civil, claim is better
(plead for us, Lord, and grant us your salvation):
there's no use going after what's not there.
Regrettably these scams are everywhere.

To save you an unnecessary journey,
please print and sign this document in full
to give me general power of attorney
unlimited and irrevocable
attested by a public notary
and stamped with Hague Convention apostille.

When I receive the deed appointing me
I'll do whatever lies within my power
to help you get your money back. My fee
is 350 pounds an hour.
Please wire retainer, non-refundable.

And may the Lord have mercy on us all.

Guy Mather's songs can be heard on Anthony Strong's CD *Guaranteed!!*

James Lever

Jonathan Glazer: Outsiders

Seven or eight minutes into Jonathan Glazer's 2000 debut, *Sexy Beast*, I suffered the wary *coup de foudre* you undergo when you first suspect you've encountered an artist you're going to love – or at least have some kind of meaningful relationship with. It's the moment where retired gangster Ray Winstone blows an uxoriously lustful smoke-ring across the terrace of his Spanish villa towards his wife Amanda Redman, and with perfectly pitched tackiness, Glazer digitally tweaks the smoke-ring into a heart. The heart then dissolves into a brief composite shot of Winstone and Redman (filmed underwater in slow-motion) floating together through the night sky above the twinkling security lights of the Costa del Crime: a glutted saurian embrace, an image of middle-aged marital bliss both satirical and celebratory, as schlocky as a velvet painting and as magical as a Chagall. The surrealism seemed no more flashily virtuosic than breathing. I was like: yeah.

In truth I was already mildly rooting for Glazer, who was one of those late-90s commercial-and-music-video directors like Michel Gondry, Spike Jonze or Chris Cunningham who made technically ultra-complex, effects-heavy promos that were funnier and more inventive, and more cinematic, than most of the movies you saw at a time (it seems a century ago) when Guy Ritchie and Danny Boyle were still being lauded for the supposedly cutting-edge energy of their kinetic styles, an energy that aped the editing mannerisms of a previous generation of music videos. In the meantime the videos were slowing down, and it was narrative that was decelerating them. Gondry and Jonze were natural fabulists – instinctively surreal, Foster Wallace-ish – the perfect fit for Charlie Kaufman's narratives. Glazer had the same story-telling reflex but without their inherent whimsy, which I felt emanated from a profound underlying gloom (I still do, but anyway). He had an eye for the indelible – he did the Guinness advert with the surfers riding the wave of CGI white horses – a fairly obvious Kubrick fixation, and his best work, like his exhaustively rewarded video for UNKLE's 'Rabbit in Your Headlights', told oblique little Kafkaesque parables. Nonetheless, since we gave the world Adrian Lyne, Tony Scott and Tony Kaye, any British advertising-*wunderkind* moving into features was likely to be accused of favouring style over content. To which *Sexy Beast*'s lightly-worn mastery felt almost like a rejoinder. Glazer's style wasn't so much economical as just plain allergic to waste: the film is 81 minutes long, but somehow has plenty of air in it. Built slyly and very funnily around a classic gangster-movie subtext (the gangsters' self-hating terror of their own latent homosexuality), it's basically Ray Winstone trying not to disintegrate in the face of Ben Kingsley and Ian McShane's scrutiny, and an invitation for an artily-minded director to claim a visual style by ODing on the close-ups. But there was no directorial signature, no camera whoop-de-do (to quote Pauline Kael on the Coens) only an unbroken series of undogmatic and attentive shots serving the story and the actors: Kingsley's turn became famous, and there simply aren't any better Winstone or McShane big-screen performances. It had the kind of restraint you get when talent isn't intoxicated with itself. That Glazer habitually played down his contribution, stating that he'd only 'pointed the camera at what the script said', was the modesty that tends to accompany artistry – a bonus.

Unfortunately, it came out slap-bang in the middle of the post-*Lock, Stock and Two Smoking Barrels* anti-renaissance of the British gangster movie, an eighteen-month infestation at the turn of the millennium which included *Snatch*, the TV show of *Lock Stock* (sponsored by *The Sun*), *Going Off Big Time* (Scousers), *Shooters* (Scousers), *Everybody Loves Sunshine* (Mancs), *Essex Boys* (Essex boys), *Rancid Aluminium* (cockneys and Russians), *Shiner* (cockneys and boxers), *Mr In-Between* (cockneys, 'arty'), *Gangster No. 1* (cockneys, 'stylish') and – I may have missed a few – *Love Honour and Obey* (mockneys, a defining nadir). In this saturated market, the natural go-to pull-quote for each movie's marketing tended to be something like 'stands head and shoulders above the average British gangster flick', a phrase which then became synonymous with the average British gangster flick – a bit of an irony for *Sexy Beast*, which was of course repeatedly underpraised as standing head and shoulders above the etc etc and never completely shed the taint of being the zenith of the geezer-pandemic, remaining, I thought, a notch or two undervalued. Glazer then developed an idea with a couple of screenwriters (including

Buñuel's old collaborator Jean-Claude Carriere) for his follow-up, *Birth* (2004). It cost $20 million, got horrible reviews and bombed.

Birth goes like this: ten years into widowhood, an Upper East Side beauty, Anna (Nicole Kidman), is about to remarry when a ten-year old boy abruptly presents himself to her as the reincarnation of her late and much beloved husband, Sean, who died of a heart-attack running in Central Park. The boy knows an astonishing amount about Sean and her, the still-raw Anna begins to believe him and, on the boy's urging, breaks with her minatory fiancé, Joseph (played like a tomb-door slamming shut by Danny Huston). But a woman named Clara (Anne Heche), Sean's old lover and his best friend's wife, confronts the boy: she knows he must have read Anna's love-letters to Sean, which Sean had passed unopened to Clara to prove he loved her more. Clara had meant to give the letters to Anna as a vicious engagement present but instead buried them in Central Park, where the boy found them. This doesn't explain how the boy knows where Sean died. Clara tells the boy, who seems absolutely convinced he is Sean, that he cannot be – because 'if you had been, you'd have come to me first'. Stricken, the boy tells Anna he's not Sean, Anna returns to Joseph and the boy wakes from the spell and becomes a well-adjusted eleven-year-old.

The movie looks like a *Three Colours: Blue*-ish coming-to-terms-with-unbearable-loss fable, that wintry genre which takes a secret pride – as Anna does herself – in the scale of grief and the power of denial. But *Birth* is a bolus of Pinteresque ironies. Since Sean never read Anna's letters he could hardly respond to their contents, meaning that his wife was writing into a void. Yet what she writes is a description of a marriage so profoundly blissful the boy is enchanted by it. She must have been in a state of denial bordering on insanity. Sean must have hated her – handing over her letters is an act of staggeringly needless malice – so why couldn't he leave her? Because, we suspect, Anna was already so hysterically dependent on him it would have been dangerous to do so. Then you remember that we first meet her at Sean's grave, asking his permission to remarry – talking to a void again – while her fiancé indulgently attends her decision. It's the kind of well-behaved cinematic image of closure one assents to, buttressed by the sombre elegance of the shot, the affluent gravitas of the characters – but imagine someone doing it to you and you see the gesture for the smug and spooky charade it is. Loss may well have infantilised Anna, who chews her nails, pouts, simpers and is still sore about being told there isn't a Santa Claus, but fifteen years earlier, she and Sean married each other 30 times in 30 days, another hubristic, movie-ish excess – so they were always a childishly ostentatious 'great love'. Maybe they were just *awful.* Now Anna's mother (Lauren Bacall), Joseph's sponsor, begins to seem less like a responsible parent trying to push her daughter back into life than a battle-weary combatant keen to pass on the problem. And the vampiric Joseph dwindles into a lovestruck sap suckered into a lifetime of care for an invalid.

Under examination, the movie becomes several different films simultaneously. It's never incoherent or even obscure, but every corner of it is legible in several very contradictory ways. All its adult characters exist suspended in an indeterminate limbo between their various possible pasts and futures, like Nabokov's beloved dead in *Speak, Memory*, 'silent, bothered, strangely depressed, quite unlike their dear, bright selves'. Any attempted connection between these people would be hopelessly uncertain. Set against this is the clarity and conviction of the kid. 'I'm Sean,' he keeps saying. 'I love you. You're my wife.' He exists among these shadows with the vividness and fixity of the actual. And the saddest irony in the film is that the little-boy-as-Sean is charming, kind and deeply in love with Anna, as if the man she addressed her unread letters to has returned in an immaculate (or invented) form and is trying to repent – that is, she herself has possessed the kid with her inaccurate version of Sean. *Birth*, uninterested in reincarnation or possession, is largely about the horror of the idea of a soul. Or about the terrible paralysis that idea contains, figured in Anna's arrested development and the way that it has ramified through the movie. And there's also the horror of the world if such a thing as a soul should not exist: in the final scene, Anna wanders into the ocean in her wedding dress, unable to commit suicide, unable to live. Joseph coaxes her back out of the surf and along the beach and as they grow smaller in the shot, Anna's white dress against the white sand makes her disappear from sight, as if to say: this person can only cease to be. If she does have an eternal soul it's broken, and she can only continue if she discards the notion of it. It's an earned bleakness, rarest of things.

The directing was pared down and composed but never the sort of film-making that, as David Thomson once said of Kieslowski, 'thinks it's so perfect I want to scream'. It was jokeless but not humourless, sometimes as rapturous as Ophuls, and thrumming with dread: Glazeresque, though Glazeresque plainly contained a whole bunch of Kubrickian. The opening tracking shot of Sean running to his death through Central Park was a masterpiece in itself: Sean is black against the snow, but he stays such a consistent distance from the following camera that after a while it begins, weirdly, to look like an effects-shot, a silhouette running on the spot digitally inserted into a moving landscape: that's life, running but going nowhere, and then you die. There's a renowned two-minute close-up of Kidman watching the overture to *Die Walküre* at the Met, her mind scrambled by the possibility of Sean's return, which is both one of the great close-ups and a brilliant joke on the hopelessness of trying to understand, or convey, someone's emotions from a two-minute close-up. (It's a close-up of someone trying to decode someone else's facial expression. In a touch of genius, Anna keeps flinching as Joseph leans over to *explain the plot* to her.) Nicole Kidman has a monologue where Anna tries to rationalise to Clara's husband what has happened without sounding insane but can't repress a coy pride in the little-boy-as-Sean's love for her, and you watch her horror as she hears this and realises it's the sound of her own mind slipping. It is the apex of Kidman's career.

The thing was full of jewels. I was like: woah. I thought it was, at least, the best film made by a British director in the 2000s. And people *hated* it. Venice booed it. The Tomatometer looked like the village stocks. Maybe *Birth*'s satire of 5th Avenue airlessness came over like the movie's own frigidity, or maybe, having set out like *Rosemary's Baby* or *The Shining* or *The Exorcist*, it was too anticlimactic for it then to turn into something closer to *Cries and Whispers* or Dreyer's *Ordet*. It was an arthouse picture that came on like a mainstream one, and neither liked it. Its actual genre, I hoped, was that kind of oblique, and always beautiful, psychological thriller which on release is described as 'elegant claptrap' or something similar (the elegance allegedly a misdirection while the claptrap tries to burgle your unconscious) and which then ages disturbingly well, as if there is after all something occult about the way you've been beguiled. Which there is. *Vertigo* was an elegant claptrap movie in its day, so was *The Tenant*, even *Don't Look Now* – films which, like *Birth*, concern muffled or inarticulate attempts at communication by the past. It suits these movies to call to us across time – they become, over the years, ever more like themselves.

Glazer then went quiet. In 2005 he made his best ever video, for Massive Attack's *Live With Me*, but the golden era of music promos had gone. He did a number of ads including one for Cadbury's Flake which was withdrawn for being overly fellatial (one wonders what the brief was) but otherwise nothing: he was supposed to be working on an adaptation of Michel Faber's *Under the Skin*, about a woman who murders hitch-hikers along the A9 in Scotland and turns out to be an alien whose species considers human flesh a delicacy, whereupon the book declines from an inspired thriller to a satire about intensive farming and the ethics of meat-consumption. It seemed either unadaptable or just wildly ambitious. The rest of the decade passed, and what had promised to be a career of Kubrickian variety began to look like one of Malickian aporia.

However, in Glazer's absence (and with Shane Meadows becalmed and Michael Winterbottom inconsistent) *Birth*'s reputation was growing. Gradually, it began to be prefaced with 'the divisive'. After a while it graduated to 'the underrated'. By the time *Under the Skin* finally, after many script iterations, started shooting in 2011, Glazer was in that peculiar place: he was a guy whom everybody thought was underrated. Which meant his next work would be overrated. Nine years to the week after the same audience had jeered *Birth*'s difficult birth, what was now being referred to as Glazer's comeback (but comeback to what?) was ready to premiere at the 2013 Venice Film Festival. I thought what the hell, it's Venice, and went.

And what a pleasure, to take the boat across the lagoon to the Lido every morning, your accreditation flapping in the breeze, and to make the very cinematic slow zoom down the canal, lined with oleanders and virid with iridescent seaweed, that leads you to the Palazzo del Cinema. And then how weird and counterintuitive to go and huddle in the dark. As I lounged on the beach between movies in that pleasantly drunk Venetian disequilibrium – wobbly from vaporetti – and further scrambled by the tumbling *Gravity* (or maybe I was just pleasantly drunk), I worried that I was a little over-invested in *Under The Skin*. I could feel a bile of vindication, thirteen years in the brewing, slopping around inside me, and some internal screenwriter seemed to be talentlessly constructing a redemptive Glazer biopic in my head, opening with the Venetians booing *Birth* and closing with Bertolucci (this year's jury president) tearfully awarding *Under The Skin* the Golden Lion – perhaps I should buttonhole Harvey Weinstein, busily visible on the terrace of the Hotel Superior, and pitch it to him? All very shaming. But I did care about Glazer, in part because I thought he was interested in a mainstream audience at a time when the arthouse increasingly declined to be. *Birth* was risky in a way that Glazer's most lionised compatriots were not: Steve McQueen, Lynne Ramsay, Andrea Arnold, Joanna Hogg, contentedly bedded down in a would-be Bressonian aesthetic that easily shrinks to that familiar commute between grimness and transcendence. They were, in a word, safe: secure in ambiguity, quarantined well away from the difficulties of humour and cossetted by an obsolete critical lexicon that still unblushingly uses 'unflinching' and 'brave' to describe the orthodox contemporary festival-circuit style, where maximum freedom of interpretation is a non-negotiable aesthetic ideal that habitually coarsens into taciturnity, a grudging of meaning. (It may be worth noting that Ramsay's shot at a larger audience, *We Need To Talk About Kevin*, is by far her most uncertain film. And whatever the merits of McQueen's step-up, *12 Years*

A Slave, its subject and especially structure render it the least daring or exposing project conceivable for its director.) In comparison to their uncommunicative formalism, *Birth*'s obscurity felt like the girl on the beach at the end of *La Dolce Vita*, trying with all her heart to signify something to Marcello and failing, but not for want of effort or something to say, and not entirely.

Anyway, coffee, vaporetto, Palazzo del Cinema, front of the queue and at last, the return of the underrated prodigal, which of course – you're way ahead of me – turned out to be implacably opaque and viewer-resistant and utterly unbothered by any mainstream sensibility. Rather uncertain boos greeted its conclusion, like the first speculative threads lobbed over Gulliver. 'It's *The Woman Who Fell To Earth*!' one fan was trying out on the steps outside. 'More like *The Director Who Fell To Earth*,' someone else grumbled. Great, five minutes old and it was already a cult film. I was like – wait, what *was* I like? Glazer and co-writer Walter Campbell, his old partner from adverts and videos, had shucked everything but the central conceit (and the final paragraph) from Faber's text, leaving us with Scarlett Johansson as not necessarily an alien, just *something* clothed in a human integument, driving a van around Glasgow and the Scottish countryside in search of men to seduce, abduct, store and, in an abstract yet very frightening way, harvest. Almost imperceptibly this being develops an empathy for humanity, evolving, in Glazer's words, 'from an it to a she'. It/she frees one of her abductees and heads out to explore the world with her ever-more human senses before ending violently, another victim of our species. And even this cautious synopsis feels over-determined: 'empathy', for instance, may well be wrong.

Conceptually, it's sort of brilliant: Glazer fitted Johansson's van with hidden cameras and left her to drive around Glasgow, picking up actual male passers-by and flirting with them: these are the people we see in the film. So imagine, this incredible girl who looks like Scarlett Johansson, though her hair is black, offers you a lift and starts coming on to you. She's dressed like you, like a working-class Govanite, but talks in a posh-yet-approachable-dream-girl London accent (a great touch); she's funny and warm; she's yours. Then suddenly she tells you she really is Scarlett Johansson and you are in fact in a movie. At this moment, as men with release-forms come trotting up and the unattainable international sex-symbol/movie-star replaces the girl you thought was yours, you might feel like your own desire has been used as a weapon against you – which is exactly what the alien does to her victims in the film, and also what any cinematic or false object of desire does to your subconscious. Your own fantasy has come alive to seduce and then mock you. And the superstar, who might as well be an alien for all the chance you stand with her, has left you hollowed out – enacting what the fiction will.

In the alien's lair – an abstract, ideally black space, like sexual tunnel-vision – the creature's victims, naked and erect, approach the flirtatiously retreating Johansson; as they get close, the floor turns liquid and they sink painlessly into the black, still walking, uncomprehending. There they will be stored and then surreally emptied in an instant, leaving only a husk of skin that resembles, as someone observed, a used condom. These (astounding) sequences, very beautiful in contrast to the *verité* footage of Glasgow, seem like a portrait of the frightening glamour of movies – the black is a lustrous *noir*, glossy like celluloid, the music a mesmeric Bernard Herrmann-ish snake-dance, the *femme fatale* recedes even as she undresses, and the ordinary man who might literally be you is entranced, then engulfed, then ruined by it all.

But the movie's not soliciting that kind of reading. (Plus, if the movie's not about cinema itself, it's either about the male gaze or surveillance, right? That's a rule.) It's more like a dispassionate nature programme that happens to feature humans: 'So much of the film,' Glazer wrote in a brief email interview, 'was trying to film nothing more than behaviour. Or instinct, maybe. Appetite.' Within the general swirl of biological imperatives the anomalous kindness of humans becomes the film's focus. Its greatest passage (where, not coincidentally, Glazer allows his gift for narrative to flow) takes place on a stony beach, where the alien is grooming a tourist from the Czech Republic to be her next victim. Suddenly he bolts. We see why: a dog's struggling in the heavy swell. Then we notice with horror that there's a woman in the surf, trying to rescue her dog and in deep trouble. The woman's husband swims out to rescue her and himself begins to flounder. And then the Czech dives in to save the husband (who breaks away to try and save his wife, or die with her). This is an unbearably sad short story about the nature of altruism and love that is only complete when you realise that the now drowned couple have left their baby crying on the shore. Which Johansson leaves to the gulls. (Glazer: 'You try and put things in front of her that mean something to us and wait to see if there's an equivalent reaction from her. And there never is. And there's the alien.')

Later, when she stumbles and falls on the street and kindly Glaswegians (unaware of the camera) rush like white blood cells to her, a chain reaction of human emotion is set in motion – pain and vulnerability lead to gratitude, empathy, pity, affection, doubt, fear, etc, as if she has contracted a runaway fever of humanity, which kills her in the end. Glazer's description is: 'It's like she gets into still waters and ends up being carried by the current into rapids.' Maybe it's the director's innate brilliance, even genius, with a kind of intensely coloured *noir* aesthetic (he belongs in a Hitchcock/Antonioni/Lynch/Roeg tradition) or his reflex creation of an immanent sense of dread, but this alien seemed to me to be a sister of one of Hitchcock's guilty runaways – she's like *Psycho*'s Marion Crane or, especially, Marnie, who was seductive but frigid, who compulsively castrated men by stealing from them, who was a virgin, was raped, and wanted to die. That's what happens to the alien. Then again, she might as well be Audrey Hepburn in *Roman Holiday*, quitting her job in search of real feelings, or Arnold in T-2, learning the thumbs-up. Who knows? You simply cannot read what she's thinking. And that's that. She is impenetrable – just like her body and just like, in the end, the movie.

At the press conference, Glazer dismissed a question about *Under The Skin*'s themes with a rather scoffing, 'Love, sex, life, death...you can analyse it for me'. And though daring to ask any contemporary arthouse film-maker about his or her themes is a *bêtise* equivalent to asking *Don't Look Back*-era Dylan about protest songs, this seemed a disappointingly Swintonian reply. *Et tu, Jonathan*? I muttered. Here we were, back in the position of maximum freedom of interpretation, where the expressive close-ups express nothing (and this being a film festival, I'd been supping all week on charged silence). But he was also right: *Under The Skin* doesn't really have or need themes in the way of current experimental darlings *Holy Motors* (Leos Carax, 2010), Gaspar Noé's *Enter The Void* (2012) or Shane Carruth's *Upstream Color* (2013) – films to which it'll be compared. Variously radical in approach but surprisingly uniform and sentimental in their sensibility, these anti-narratives' ellipses and discontinuities all eventually lead to the same place – wonderment. They're 'Life is...' movies. In them, life is weird (Carax), empty (Noé) or sad (Carruth), but always also wonderful, and always a dream, and always cyclical – a clue to the films' desire to be infinitely rewatchable, and also to their philosophical passivity and woolliness. In contrast, *Under The Skin*, for all its opacity, is bracingly specific and direct. (And daringly non-nonlinear.) I watched it three times, and it doesn't really have secrets to yield up or connections to tease out: it doesn't court repeat viewing in that audience-flattering way puzzle-movies do. The impenetrability here isn't a by-product of narrative undernourishment or a desire to be maximally suggestive but rather an intensification of the preoccupation Glazer has nursed all his career, whether trying to understand Ben Kingsley or trying to figure out if the little boy is actually Sean. Rarely will you feel such aggressive resistance to exegesis pushing back at you, like an active force. That's both the affect of the alien and Glazer's main theme. His three films are about the inconceivable, come tapping on our windowpane, trying to get in where it's warm. They are inconceivably hostile things – a psychopath, a lost soul, a *thing* – but also inconceivably pitiful.

Maybe I just like him. During my time in Venice, I visited the Biennale by mistake and, wandering through the pavilions and among the sad, mute objects that littered their floors like luggage scattered from a plane crash, or children abandoned in a Chinese dying room, I listened to their silence and wished I was in the *Accademia* with Giorgione's close-mouthed, ungraspable, but very movie-ish *Tempest* (an elegant claptrap picture if ever there was one), a better quality of charged silence. Glazer's silences thrum like Rachel Whiteread casts. Or maybe I just like him. 'I think of film as a miracle,' he wrote, 'When you identify the right moments and put them in the right order, all their shortcomings suddenly take flight in some new glorious formation. And you follow that. That supersedes the written order you might have planned.' This may only work about 60% of the time in *Under The Skin*, but it's well said. And as for being a fan, with its attendant bellicosity, its impatience, its neediness and fretfulness, its repellent creeping sense of ownership, its obsessive-compulsive mental re-editing of imperfections – could anything be more of a drag? At my age? Enough with being a fan. Jonathan Glazer's new film is not what I was hoping for, very brilliant indeed, occasionally not that far from a folly, and I can live with that.

James Lever is the author of *Me Cheeta*, which was shortlisted for the Booker Prize in 2009.

Claire Lowdon

Kafka: Warrior Worrier

Camus's *L'étranger* begins with the famously affectless declaration: 'Aujourd'hui, Maman est morte. Ou peut-être hier, je ne sais pas.' *Mother died today. Or maybe yesterday, I don't know.* In court later, the speaker, Meursault, is arraigned for swimming on the day following her funeral.

Franz Kafka's diary entry for 2 August 1914: 'Germany has declared war on Russia – Swimming in the afternoon.'

In a novel, this juxtaposition would be significant, calculated. But here, in a diary? With Kafka, apparently, these distinctions have no purchase.

These two laconic sentences have been much pondered in the great echo chamber of Kafka commentary. They are usually taken as evidence of his insulation from real-world events, his total absorption in his own life and writings. A grand claim that sits uneasily alongside another grand claim – that his fiction predicts the horrors of World War Two concentration camps.

The hypnotic interest of the diary entry is emblematic. We tend to view Kafka's writings in hallowed isolation, as single, baffling facets of a Rosetta stone. A thing to be deciphered.

But the diary entry doesn't seem so extraordinary. Or even, as Kafka's biographer Reiner Stach believes, unintentionally comic. Set it in context. For one thing, Kafka didn't know, as we know now, exactly where Germany's declaration would lead. He was certainly politically engaged, however: he attended war rallies in Prague and sank a good proportion of his savings into government-issued 'war bonds'. So he was probably reading and talking about the ensuing conflict on a daily basis – and might therefore quite reasonably not have bothered to rehash those opinions in a diary that was not intended for public consumption. And in any case, the diary was really more of a notebook.

Not intended for public consumption. Only nine of Kafka's short stories were published during his lifetime, along with a handful of sketches. The rest of his work – including his three novels, all of which are unfinished – he asked his friend Max Brod to destroy in the event of his death. Brod ignored this request. When Kafka died from tuberculosis in 1924 at the age of 41, Brod immediately set about publishing all Kafka's 'corpus', much of which was unfinished and culled from notebooks and jottings.

Brod's decision is a complicated positive. Twentieth-century literature would certainly be the poorer without *The Trial*, for example. But it seems strange that, in Germany in 1931, the first posthumous collection of Kafka's previously unpublished short stories should include not only 'The Hunter Gracchus' but one of the fragments associated with that story. Later editions include up to four Gracchus fragments, as if they were deliberate variants – a kind of musical canon. Essentially, they are false starts, the writer's rough workings, experimenting with different voices and points of view. Their publication would surely have been abhorrent to Kafka, a perfectionist who placed great importance on selection and burned a considerable amount of his work during his lifetime.

The fragments for 'Gracchus' and other stories such as 'A Report to an Academy' are supporting drafts that would typically be reserved for academic study. Yet several were published only a decade after Kafka's death in volumes aimed at the general reader. The message was clear: here is a writer so important that even his false starts are worthy of our close attention. Thus began a steady inflation, in which every Kafkan utterance, no matter how small, has been scaled up to serve as a touchstone. A touchstone for anything: the suffering of the Jews, the brutality of the totalitarian state, the dehumanising effects of bureaucracy.

The mystique generated by Brod made Kafka's reputation. It also did him a disservice. So much is promised by the press release that the experience of reading Kafka is inevitably filtered through pre-existing expectations. Filtered – and skewed. The more difficulty and obfuscation we anticipate, the more we are likely to find. Then there are the many readers who approach his texts with trepidation and end up feeling stupid when they fail to finish them. In fact, we should be unafraid to set Kafka in context – to see him as another Modernist writer, who is part of an ongoing corrective conversation with the past. His stories are absurdist, conceptual, expressionist. They are also an extension of the realist project. Nor should we forget that much of his work is unfinished. There is elegance, wit, concision – but there is plenty of chaff as well. True, he is responsible for some of the most memorable imagery in literature, but at the level of the sentence he is often unremarkable. Sometimes he is simply boring. Not a saint, not a visionary, not infinite or infallible: just a writer, uneven if brilliant, who had his strengths and his weaknesses.

1. MY NEVERENDING IS IN MY BEGINNING

When his friend Gustav Janouch described Picasso as a 'wilful distortionist', Kafka made the following objection: 'I do not think so... He only registers the deformities which have not yet penetrated our consciousness. Art is a mirror, which goes "fast", like a watch – sometimes.'

* * *

There is scintilla of truth in the critical fallacy that all nineteenth-century novels have happy endings. Nineteenth-century novels are more likely to end neatly (be it happily or unhappily, ironically or earnestly) with a decisive event or summary which 'seals off' the narrative. With the advent of modernism, writers began pushing this tradition forwards – quite literally.

At the end of *Anna Karenina*, Levin experiences a religious epiphany and determines that from now on he'll never be unkind or irritable. Riding home immediately after this experience, he restrains himself from criticising his coachman for pulling up the saddle-girth too high. The coachman then advises Levin, who is holding the reins, to keep right to avoid a tree-stump, and Levin immediately finds himself getting cross. Over the next few pages, his resolution fails again and again.

Tolstoy is not suggesting that Levin's epiphany has been entirely unsuccessful – just that it is less complete, less final, more complicated, than Levin himself first imagines. Tolstoy has done on his character's behalf something difficult: he has looked beyond a strong, persuasive feeling, an apparently permanent situation.

Kafka was the master of looking beyond, to the next thing and the next thing and the next – not an infinite regressus, but an infinite progressus. Like Picasso, his work mirrored and exaggerated 'the deformities which have not yet penetrated our consciousness'. A central 'deformity' was this awareness of time's relentless march, the impermanence of the present moment. 'When you think it over, winning a race is nothing to sigh for,' claims the opening line of a short story entitled 'Reflections for Gentleman Jockeys.' The rest of the story, a plethora of possibilities, explains why: if you win, you'll have withdrawal symptoms from the intoxication of the applause; you'll be troubled by your envy of your opponents; many of your friends will be too caught up in the excitement of their winnings to properly congratulate you. And so on, until the self-consciously dour ending: 'Finally from the now overcast sky rain actually begins to fall.'

The unspoken conclusion is that it would be better not to win, or even to race at all. This paralysis – both comic and terrible – appears throughout Kafka's oeuvre in many different forms. Think of the endless paranoia of the creature in 'The Burrow', its inner satnav perpetually recalculating; or K, failing for 275 pages to reach the Castle; or the end of the short parable 'The Coming of the Messiah': 'The Messiah will come only when he is no longer necessary; he will come only on the day after his arrival; he will come, not on the last day, but on the very last.' Indefinite deferral. Fortune's wheel, ceaselessly spinning, reaching only the conclusion that there are no conclusions. Interesting philosophically, but problematic, as Kafka himself noted, when it came to actually finishing a piece of work. In a letter of 11 November 1912, he wrote that his first novel, *Amerika*, was 'designed in such a way that it will never have an ending'.

Tragically for those who loved him, his talent for thinking on to the next thing and the next was active in his life as well as his fiction. The letter about *Amerika* was one of three letters sent that day to Felice Bauer, the Berlin woman who would become his fiancée, twice, but never his wife. They met at a dinner party thrown by mutual friends, when Kafka was 29 and Felice 24. He was a trained lawyer employed by the Workers Accident Insurance Institute, by all accounts very good at this job, and still living at home with his parents in Prague. She was stenographer from Berlin, also living with her family. Despite an apparent absence of initial attraction, Kafka wrote to her five weeks later, initiating an intense correspondence (of which only Kafka's letters to Felice have survived). Two days after the start of this correspondence, Kafka wrote 'The Judgment', a story he considered one of the major breakthroughs of his artistic life.

It would be eight months before Kafka and Felice would meet again, and another year before they were formally engaged. Their relationship had been conducted almost entirely by post. Kafka's parents employed the services of a private detective agency to check up on Felice's background (fairly standard practice for middle-class Jews at this time) and both families gave their blessing to the union. The engagement ceremony took place in Berlin in April 1914.

Kafka was freaked by everything about the event: the announcements in the paper, the relatives openly assessing him, the meat that had been cooked in his honour, and which he refused to eat, even though he wasn't strictly vegetarian. 'Had they sat me down in a corner with real chains and posted policemen in front of me and let me look on simply like that, it could not have been worse,' he noted in his diary. A routine shopping trip to buy furniture for their new apartment in Prague was also terrifying, as he explained to Felice in a later letter: 'Heavy furniture that looked as though it could never be removed once it was in place. Its solidity is exactly what you liked most about it. My chest felt crushed by the sideboard; it was a perfect tombstone or a monument to the life of an official in Prague.'

Yet it was Felice, not Kafka, who initiated the first rupture. During the months leading up to the engagement ceremony Kafka had been writing to Felice's friend Grete Bloch. Their correspondence quickly became an emotional betrayal of Felice, if not a physical one. (A theory exists that Grete Bloch had a son by Kafka, who died in 1921, aged six; but Stach persuasively argues the lack of evidence for this claim.) Following the engagement party, Grete had an attack of conscience and showed her letters from Kafka to Felice (with anything that might incriminate her cut out). In these letters, Kafka openly expresses doubts about the engagement. He was summoned back to Berlin and on 23 July he faced a 'tribunal' in the Askanischer Hof hotel – Grete, Felice, and Felice's sister Erma. Kafka remained silent while the evidence was brought against him. According to Kafka, Felice said 'certain things that ought to be almost impossible for one person to say to another'. In a letter to Grete Bloch written on 15 October 1914, he describes Grete as sitting 'in judgment' over him.

It was around this time that he began work on *The Trial*, a fiction in which the guilt of K is a narrative assumption, not subject to appeal.

'I cannot live with you – It would be life,' wrote Emily Dickinson. In Kafka's case, the life entailed by conventional cohabitation – the financial and familial responsibilities this would bring – was something to be feared because of the danger it represented to his writing, to his 'talent for portraying my dreamlike inner life'. 'My life has dwindled dreadfully, nor will it cease to dwindle. Nothing else will ever satisfy me,' he wrote in his diary on 6 August 1914, two weeks after the split from Felice.

Kafka had foreseen the crisis at the very start of his relationship with

Felice. As well as the three letters he posted on 11 November 1912, there was a fourth letter, never sent, that forbade Felice from writing to him again: 'I would be bound to make you unhappy by writing to you, and as for me I am beyond help. To realise this I need not have counted the striking of the clock all through the night; I was well aware of it before writing my first letter to you.'

'I am made of literature. I am nothing else and cannot be anything else': it was the primacy of his writing, rather than the fear of sex commonly ascribed to him, that seems to have corroded Kafka's relationships. Often thought of as the archetypal lonely bachelor – by himself as well as others – Kafka was in fact a serial monogamist who visited brothels throughout his life. He had physical relations with at least two of his lovers – Julie Wohryzek, to whom he was briefly engaged in 1919, and Milena Jesenska, a Christian woman married to the Jewish Ernst Pollack. Milena translated some of Kafka's stories into Czech and corresponded passionately with him from April to November 1920.

It was only at the very end of his life that Kafka found in Dora Diamant a woman with whom he felt he could share a roof. Together they fulfilled his life-long dream of moving to Berlin so that he could write. He could hardly have picked a worse time for the move: it was 1923, and post-war inflation left them impoverished, cold and hungry. Kafka had been tubercular since 1917 – a diagnosis that, perversely, came as a relief. (Perhaps because, for once, something was certain, final.) 'This is a special illness,' he wrote to Felix Weltsch, 'you might say an illness bestowed on me – quite different from the others I have had to deal with previously.' And, to his beloved sister Ottla, on whose farm he spent several months of sick leave in 1917: 'There is undoubtedly justice in this illness; it is a just blow, which, incidentally, I do not feel at all as a blow, but as something quite sweet in comparison with the average course of past years.' Stach's plausible theory is that 'the tuberculosis supplied a justification for social retreat' – that is, more time for writing.

But in 1923 in Berlin, six years later, time was running down. Kafka was still working hard towards the end: 'The Burrow' was written in December 1923. He completed his last work, 'Josephine the Singer, or the Mouse Folk' in March 1924. By now, Kafka had left Berlin for Prague, but he was only at home for a few days before he was moved to Austria for treatment. In his final weeks, spent at a private sanatorium in Kierling near Vienna, he worked on the page proofs for his last collection, *A Hunger Artist*. He was suffering from tuberculosis of the larynx. The pain was so bad that he was often unable to speak, or even to swallow water. Alcohol was injected into his laryngeal nerve but the relief was only temporary, and the gaps between these unpleasant injections became shorter and shorter. The scraps of paper he used for communication poignantly record his thirst, his concern for the flowers on the window-sill, ('do you have a moment? Then please lightly spray the peonies'), his fear that he was a burden to Dora and Robert Klopstock, a medical friend helping with his care. One note recalls Felice: 'I was to have gone to the Baltic with her once (along with her girl friend), but was ashamed because of my thinness and other anxieties... She was not beautiful, but slender, fine body, which she has kept according to reports.'

On the day before he died he wrote a letter to his parents in which he suggests that he is improving but asks them to postpone their visit. 'Everything is, as I said, at the best of beginnings, but even the best beginnings don't amount to much.' He fondly reminds his father, Herman Kafka – a man by whom he felt bullied and oppressed for most of his life – of their visits to the Civilian Swimming Pool where they would share a glass of beer. In the early hours of the next day, 3 June 1924, Kafka's breathing became difficult. He asked Klopstock for a lethal dose of morphine, and, when Klopstock hesitated, argued that refusal would be tantamount to murder. Klopstock gave in and administered an opiate called Pantopon. Dora had been sent on an errand so she would miss this scene, but at the last minute Kafka changed his mind and sent the maid to bring her back. She was with him when he died.

Two volumes of Reiner Stach's biography have now been published. *Kafka: The Decisive Years* covers his life from 1910 to 1915. *Kafka: The Years of Insight* takes us from 1915 to the end of his life. A third volume, covering his childhood and early adulthood, is due out this year. Stach's job cannot have been easy, given the quantity of material – the diaries, the notebooks, the letters to Felice, Milena, his family, his friends – to be digested and synthesised. Then there is all the fiction, which so often invites parallels with the life: the novels, starring Karl and then K and then again, K; the overbearing father-figures that seem to mirror Hermann Kafka; those stories that deal explicitly with the act of writing, such as 'The Giant Mole' and 'Josephine the Singer, or the Mouse Folk'. As Stach notes, even the myth-like 'The Hunter Gracchus' doesn't escape the K-stamp: *Gracchio* is the Italian word for jackdaw, which in Czech is *kavka*; Hermann Kafka used the bird as the business logo for his fancy goods store.

Stach begins with an introduction musing on the nature of biography.

He sounds openly intimidated: 'How much can a biographer afford to simplify? How far can a biographer go to reconstruct the bits and pieces in order to recount them? The sheer number of interrelations between the thematic honeycomb cells makes any narrative geometry impossible.' A life is lived, he argues, not in a line but in four dimensions, with several 'themes' coexisting at any one time. He is commendably wary of inventing, of 'filling in the gaps', and daunted by the idea of deploying words to describe the life of a man who used language so well himself.

The biography is valuable for the prodigious research on display – into Kafka's own writings but also the life and writings of almost anyone with whom he came into contact. The analyses of the fiction are mostly sensible and clear. You sense throughout Stach's great respect and enthusiasm for his subject. But anyone who makes it through both volumes will surely find it hard to agree with John Banville (*New York Review of Books*, 'A Different Kafka', 24 October 2013), when he labels this 'one of the great literary biographies'. For three reasons. The first is that Stach has supplemented Kafka's story with the history of Prague during the First World War. The idea, presumably, is to recreate the socio-historical milieu in which Kafka lived. But the weighting is wrong; there are pages and pages on new warfare technology, on the role of women in the war, on epistolary culture at the time. Often, Kafka himself disappears in a storm of questionably relevant detail.

Another frustrating feature of Stach's style is a tendency to 'novelise' the material, dropping us in *in media res* at the start of each chapter, always coming out on a cliff-hanger. This doesn't generate interest; it merely confuses. A favourite technique is to quote a chunk of text without saying who wrote it for another half-paragraph or so. You find yourself constantly scanning forwards, reaching for a handhold. His efforts at scene-setting are often distracting rather than atmospheric: 'On Saturday, September 28, a warm, sunny autumn day, Kafka strode through the *deserted* corridors of the Worker's Accident Insurance Institute *humming a tune*.' [My italics, in hushed awe of Stach's telepathic powers.]

Most problematic is Stach's attempt to render Kafka's life in four dimensions, as a 'thematic honeycomb'. In a biography of over 1000 pages and counting, a clear linear narrative, however artificial, is essential. Treating his material thematically, Stach shuttles back and forth in time, telling each event three times from different angles. As if narrative progress were the responsibility of a knight in chess – dressage rather than directness.

2. FEELING

On 5 September 2012, the *TLS* published an essay by Gabriel Josopovici entitled 'Why We Don't Understand Kafka'. 'We are probably no nearer to understanding ['The Judgment'] or any of his other works today than his first readers were, nor should we expect to be,' intones Josopovici's first paragraph. This is an extreme expression of an attitude that permeates Kafka criticism. The desire to ascribe Kafka's work the status of an ineffable mystery seems strangely religious: he is hallowed ground, the exception to every rule. For example, David Foster Wallace baulks at the irony of performing 'standard undergrad-course literary analysis' on a Kafka story: it would be 'the literary equivalent of tearing the petals off and grinding them up and running the goo through a spectrometer to explain why a rose smells so pretty'. (*Harper's*, July 1998.)

Even Zadie Smith, in her clever and stunningly well-read essay on Kafka for the *New Republic* ('The Limited Circle is Pure', 3 November 2003), frames Kafka as a unique literary case. Perhaps taking her inspiration from a *deleted* Zürau aphorism – 'No more psychology ever again!' – she writes: 'Kafka is the exception. He has no interest in psychology, not as something that individuates our tastes, desires, needs, opinions.' His prose, she claims, 'rejects so many of the "things of the novel": its tools, tricks, machinery. It is as if he is at war with the novel itself.'

What are the novel's 'tools, tricks, machinery'? Crudely: description, character, plot or narrative structure. And to an extent, it is true that Kafka eschews these things. But he is not the only novelist to do so (think of Sterne, think of Beckett) and it is not so straightforward as a total rejection.

Let's take them one at a time, starting with description. Obviously there is plenty of precise description in Kafka's fiction – of the effects of Gregor Samsa's horrible metamorphosis, for example, or the Harrow in 'In the Penal Colony'. And it is Kafka's genius to make these unreal things feel real. But when he confines himself to traditional novelistic territory – the concrete world, as we experience it every day – his descriptive powers are decidedly weaker. Here is a street scene at the start of 'Wedding Preparations in the Country':

> On the pavement straight in front of him there were many people walking in various rhythms. Every now and again one would step forward and cross the road. A little girl was holding a tired puppy in her outstretched hands. Two

> gentlemen were exchanging information. The one held his hands palm-upward, raising and lowering them in regular motion, as though he were balancing a load. Then one caught sight of a lady whose hat was heavily laden with ribbons, buckles, and flowers.

Nothing is actually wrong here, but the frigid prose is unremarkable, a dutiful stacking-up of details. There is not one image to lay against Joyce's pavements in *Ulysses*, with the 'flabby gush of porter' floating up from Larry O'Rourke's cellar grating, the 'shiny links packed with forcemeat' in the butcher's window, a shopper's 'vigorous hips'. When his realism isn't magical, Kafka too often belongs to the flat-pack school of description, as practised by Ivy Compton-Burnett ('Duncan Edgeworth was a man of medium height and build, appearing both to others and himself to be tall. He had narrow, grey eyes, stiff, grey hair and beard, a solid, aquiline face, young for his sixty-six years, and a stiff, imperious bearing. His wife was a small, spare, sallow woman...' (*A House And Its Head*)).

Every writer is forced to work with what (s)he has to hand. Perhaps the reason that there aren't more brilliant descriptions of butter-dishes in Kafka's fiction is less a rejection of butter-dish description than a tacit acknowledgement that he wasn't particularly brilliant at it: the shrewd avoidance of a shortcoming.

Next up, character. Smith's claim that Kafka's work is about 'the psychology of only one man' seems a little extreme when you consider, say, Gregor Samsa's sister in 'The Metamorphosis'. The story is third-person focalised for Gregor; his experience is central. But the narrative of the sister's attitude to his transformation is subtly yet sharply drawn. At first, she is frightened and repulsed. Then, when she gets used to the idea that the bug is really her brother, she takes pity on him and overcomes her revulsion sufficiently to provide him with food, and even to ascertain, by trial and error, exactly what it is he likes to eat. After a few weeks of living with a giant bug, however, she starts to harden against him; he seems less and less like Gregor; he becomes a nuisance, and when he finally dies, she feels it as a relief. Her portrait is unsentimental and completely convincing.

Several of Kafka's shorter stories are little studies in psychology. Here is 'Rejection' in its entirety:

> When I meet a pretty girl and beg her: 'Be so good as to come with me,' and she walks past without a word, this is

what she means to say:

> 'You are no Duke with a famous name, no broad American with a Red Indian figure, level, brooding eyes and a skin tempered by the air of the prairies and the rivers that flow through them, you have never journeyed to the seven seas and voyaged on them wherever they may be, I don't know where. So why, pray, should a pretty girl like myself go with you?'
>
> 'You forget that no automobile swings you through the street in long thrusts; I see no gentlemen escorting you in a close half-circle, pressing on your skirts from behind and murmuring blessings on your head; your breasts are well laced into your bodice, but your thighs and hips make up for that restraint; you are wearing a taffeta dress with a pleated skirt such as delighted all of us last autumn, and yet you smile – inviting mortal danger – from time to time.'
>
> 'Yes, we're both in the right, and to keep us from being irrevocably aware of it, hadn't we better just go our separate ways home?'

For Smith, this is a 'nasty little parable' in which two young people 'imagine the entire relationship, imagine the pain that would result, and decide not to bother'. This isn't quite right. In fact, the focus is on the retaliatory nature of rejection: our speaker, the man, is interested until he senses the contempt in the girl's silent dismissal, which he then answers with contempt of his own. No one even begins to imagine a relationship. The humour lies in the swift bile of the speaker's reassessment: at first, he wanted her, but now he can see that she's got a big arse and her skirt's a bit passé. Sharp, funny, accurate – and not actually that radical at all. 'Rejection' is a piece of satirical observation that would feel right in a Jane Austen novel.

Smith again: 'The peculiar beauty of Kafka lies in the very impossibility of his project, which was, I think, to express concretely – in the most precise language available – those things in life that fall outside of the concretely explicable or expressible.' And once again: yes, to an extent. The subconscious, dream, emotion, atmosphere, incoherence, meaninglessness – Kafka was interested in all these things, and all these things 'fall outside of the concretely explicable and expressible'. But he is not alone in his interest. As Kundera notes in *The Art of the Novel*, 'all novels, of every age, are concerned with the enigma of the self'. And the best novelists are all working to express 'concretely – in the most precise language available' things which have not yet been expressed.

Kafka's innovation was to isolate and exaggerate the nebulousness of existing in the world. Minor emotions – usually a side-dish, with coherent motivation as the main – are foregrounded: one thing we often know for certain in *The Trial* is what Josef K is feeling. In *Madame Bovary*, Flaubert ironised the romantic novel's obsession with heightened emotions. Kafka develops this project by working with an emotional palette that is unusually drab and therefore unusually realistic. K spends most of *The Trial* confused or annoyed. Other favourite feelings include indignation, superiority, agitation, irritation, entitlement, offence, worry, responsibility, detachment, surprise, anger, diffidence. K is a feeling being but an uncomprehending one, desperately trying to make sense of a meaningless world. The human condition, but on steroids.

Finally, we come to narrative structure. Zadie Smith: 'If part of what it is to be a novel (rather than a collection of short stories) is to have significant sequence in a narrative, then Kafka's miraculous novels fail to fulfill one of the novel's defining criteria.' A novelist selects, arranges, orders – but though Kafka's novels are full of dead-ends and non-sequiturs, his nonsense makes sense. Kafka is writing about the essential formlessness of human existence, so a disordered narrative is in itself a significant sequence. This too can be seen as an extension and an exaggeration of what had come before. (The mirror of art, going fast like a watch.) Kafka is by no means the first writer to disrupt the chain of cause and effect – he just takes that disruption to its absolute extreme. Think of Fagin on trial in *Oliver Twist*, counting the spikes round the dock, being distracted by the broken pencil point of the court artist.

3. DREAMING / READING / MEANING

In dream, Kafka found the perfect objective correlative for his particular view of life. The diaries are full of dreams, which he was able to remember in detail. It is worth reproducing part of one, to show just how close these entries lie to his fiction:

> Dreams: In Berlin, through the streets to her house, calm and happy in the knowledge that, though I haven't arrived

> at her house yet, a slight possibility of doing so exists; I shall certainly arrive there. I see the streets, on a white house a sign, something like 'The Splendours of the North' (saw it in the paper yesterday); in my dream 'Berlin W' has been added to it. Ask the way of an affable, red-nosed old policeman who in this instance is stuffed into a sort of butler's livery. Am given excessively detailed directions, he even points out the railing of a small park in the distance which I must keep hold of for safety's sake when I go past. Then advice about the tram-car, the U-Bahn, etc. I can't follow him any longer and ask in a fright, knowing full well that I am underestimating the distance: 'That's about half an hour away?' But the old man answers, 'I can make it in six minutes.' What joy! Some man, a shadow, a companion, is always at my side, I don't know who it is. Really I have no time to turn around, to turn sideways. [13 February 1914]

So many trademark features of Kafka's fiction are contained in this short extract: the rapid transitions from calmness to fright to joy, the labyrinthine backdrop that makes it impossible for the hero to reach his destination, the warping of space and/or time in his conversation with the policeman… In fact, were Brod still with us, he could remove the words 'Dream' and '(saw it in the papers yesterday)', slap on a title, and we'd have a new Kafka story, 'The U-Bahn'.

Although dreams were Kafka's raw material, the word 'dream' is notable in his oeuvre for its absence or negation. There is a short story called 'The Dream', which features Joseph K in a cemetery, but otherwise references to sleep and dream seem to be deliberate attempts to put us off the scent. In Kafka, characters are always waking up, often out of dreams. The opening of 'The Metamorphosis': 'As Gregor Samsa awoke one morning from uneasy dreams…' And a short while later: 'What has happened to me? he thought. It was no dream.' It is a calculated evasion that greatly contributes to his fiction's uncanny power. For comparison, we have Gombrowicz's *Ferdydurke*, in which the adult protagonist wakes up to find himself trapped in the body of an adolescent schoolboy. *Ferdydurke* is much more explicit about its own dream-like qualities: 'I thought I was dreaming – because it is in a dream that we fall into a situation more stupid than anything we could imagine.' Compared to Kafka, this is clumsy. The poker face is crucial.

It is partly that poker face and partly a love of difficulty that prevents so many critics from reaching for the dream-solution. Consider this passage from 'A Description of A Struggle':

> I happily spread out my arms in order to fully enjoy the moon. And by making swimming movements with my weary arms it was easy for me to advance without pain or difficulty. To think that I had never tried this before!

Josopovici offers the following contorted explanation: 'This indeed seems to be an example of levitation, and Leavitt, enlisting Steiner and Blavatsky, explains that we are in the presence of an "ether-body", which is the true body, not the physical body we carry around with us.' But anyone who has had the pleasure of flying in a dream will instantly recognise this as a deft description of that state – the similarity to swimming, the astonished sense of ease. Likewise, the meandering, unfinished 'Wedding Preparations in the Country' becomes much more navigable – and much funnier – when you realise that it is in fact an anxiety dream, of the sort you might have before waking to catch a plane. The protagonist – the dreamer – must travel to the country to meet his future wife, but he repeatedly misses trams, decides it's too late to travel, calculates that he can still get there in time if he leaves the next day…

Yet Kafka's stories are by no means 'just dreams' – which is why he is careful to disguise their origin. Dreaming in Kafka provides an objective correlative for the experience of living. As readers, we are placed in the position of the 'dreamer': we know as little as the protagonist does about the dream-situation. The experience of reading Kafka can be one of constant re-adjustment and reassessment, running to keep up, bending to fit. Often, this experience is shared by the protagonist. Here is K in *The Castle*, being surprised by nightfall:

> To his amazement it was already completely dark. Had he been gone so long? Surely only one, say two hours, by his reckoning. And it had been morning when he left... 'Short days, short days,' he said to himself as he slid off the sledge and walked towards the inn.

'Short days, short days' – K's feeble explanation for the darkness he doesn't understand. Kafka's texts are littered with verbs like 'seemed not to' and 'appeared to be': the protagonist squinting at the dream-world, locked into a futile, never-ending quest for understanding.

Here is K again, this time in *The Trial*:

> Only now did K. notice that the room, in which there had been only a wash-tub the last time he was there, was now a fully furnished living-room. The woman saw his surprise and said: 'Yes, we live here rent-free, but we have to clear the furniture out on days when sessions are held. My husband's job has many disadvantages.'

The dream-world responds to K's surprise and swiftly offers up a placatory rationale. On one level, this is an accurate depiction of dream – of how determined our minds are that the nonsense should make sense. But its absurdity also stands for the absurdity of the way we rationalise the real world. 'The way is infinitely long,' runs one of Kafka's aphorisms, 'nothing of it can be subtracted, nothing added, and yet everyone applies his own childish yardstick to it.' Kafka's dream-narratives mimic the unseen incoherency of real life: we see in close-up, in yardsticks, and for a sentence or two, the world makes sense. But when you pan out – or fast-forward, as Kafka seemed so helplessly bound to do – you see only confusion and mess. 'The truth,' Kafka wrote, 'is always an abyss.'

Central to the success of Kafka's fiction is how *ordinary* his dream-worlds feel. *Alice's Adventures in Wonderland*, with its grinning cats and hookah-smoking caterpillars, is an LSD-induced trip compared to *The Trial*. The Kafkan dream-world, with its drifting sense of unease, captures the real feel of dream much more accurately. ('But even more surprising, without one quite knowing what was surprising about it, was the right-hand corner...' thinks K of yet another dreary, confusing room in *The Castle*). Arguably, this is harder to do well, just as, for George Eliot, a real animal is harder to draw than a mythical one:

> The pencil is conscious of a delightful facility in drawing a griffin — the longer the claws, and the larger the wings, the better; but that marvellous facility which we mistook for genius is apt to forsake us when we want to draw a real unexaggerated lion.

It is because Kafka's dream-worlds are so lifelike that they simultaneously expose the dreamlike quality of real life.

However, this proximity – to mundane dream and to mundane real life – carries a risk. Oscar Wilde is supposed to have said that the most frightening words in the English language are 'I had a very interesting dream last night'. It is true that much of *The Castle* displays Kafka's masterful command of his personal brand of dream-logic. It is also true that after a while, the experience of reading this dream-logic loses a good deal of its charm.

Everything makes elegant conceptual sense: Josef K is working towards some unspecified goal, represented by the mysterious Castle; his attempts to reach the Castle are confused, frustrated, sidelined; and – in Kafka's projected ending – he dies without ever reaching that goal. On his death bed, Kafka proposed K be informed that his 'legal claim to live in the village was not valid, yet, taking certain auxiliary circumstances into account, he was permitted to live and work there'. So: a metaphor describing our need for an illusory sense of direction, made vivid by extended exaggeration of that dream-state where you have an urgent feeling there's something you need to do, somewhere you need to be, but you're never quite sure what, or indeed why.

275 pages of that dream is a powerful illustration of these ideas, but there are insufficient local pleasures to really sustain interest. This problem is also, perhaps especially, true of some of his less dreamy works. 'Josephine the Singer, or the Mouse Folk'; 'The Village Schoolmaster, or the Giant Mole'; even 'The Great Wall of China' – all depend on the accrual of a series of negations, a baroque destabilising of every assertion until nothing is knowable for certain. In 'Josephine the Singer,' anyone who has not heard Josephine sing 'does not know the power of song'. Yet 'Josephine's singing, as singing, is nothing out of the ordinary'. And yet, our narrator wonders, 'is it singing at all? Is it not perhaps just a piping?'. Yet 'if you sit down before her it is not merely a piping'.... Three pages of this doubling, trebling, sextupling back would be quite enough, but the story is sixteen long pages long. There is something impressive in Kafka's ability to sustain this sort of thing. It is demanding and intricate like a problem in arithmetic, where the cubic-capacity of a bath simultaneously fills with different volumes from the hot and cold taps, while emptying at different rates from the over-flow and the plug-hole. Impressive – but not exactly spectator sport.

* * *

Another parallel between reader and dreamer: both are isolated figures. We are never more alone than when we are dreaming; it is the ultimate act of solipsism, in which we inhabit a world of our own invention. ('We live, as we dream, alone': Conrad's *Heart of Darkness*.) Kafka is fascinated by loneliness. The war cry of E M Forster's *Howards End* is 'only connect!' Kafka's mission is to show, over and over again, the impossibility of ever really doing so. Or, perhaps more accurately: connections can be made (often, in his works, via sex), but they are so temporary as to be negligible. ('When you think it over, winning a race is nothing to sigh for…'). Those writers who claim that the purpose of reading is to feel less alone (Franzen, Lethem, Foster Wallace) would surely be an anathema to Kafka.

Kafka's stories are full of crowds. An example from *The Trial*:

> K had the impression he was walking into a great assembly. A crowd of the most varied people – *nobody bothered about the one who now came in* – packed a medium-sized room with a gallery running round just under the ceiling, this too filled with people who could stand only in a bent posture, their heads and backs pressed against the ceiling. [my italics]

The function of these faceless crowds, who always act and react as a single organism, is to highlight the aloneness of K – and to dangle the promise of communion, of life in the village, yet never allow admittance.

Isolation from others is something that Kafka seems to associate with age. Several of his protagonists, while not elderly, are in their thirties and concerned about being unmarried, about facing old age alone. Children, however, are able to achieve communion. The short story 'Children on a Country Road' offers us a rare view of the crowd from the inside:

> We sang much faster than the train was going, we waved our arms because our voices were not enough, our voices rushed together in an avalanche of sound that did us good When one joins in song with others it is like being drawn on by a fish hook.

By adolescence, the bliss of communion has faded and the isolating frustrations of adult life are visible on the horizon. In 'The Refusal', all the adults in 'our little town' are resigned to life's pointless cycle of expectation and refusal. But, the narrator notes, there is 'a certain age group that is not content':

> These are the young people roughly between seventeen and twenty. Quite young fellows, in fact, who are utterly incapable of foreseeing the consequences of even the least significant, far less a revolutionary, idea. And it is just among them that the discontent creeps in.

The Trial opens on K's thirtieth birthday, when K is placed under arrest by a mysterious court for an unnamed crime. For the rest of the novel, he works on his case, attempting to defend and acquit himself. Stach notes Kafka's manuscript revisions: 'Kafka meticulously deleted any indication of independent activity on the part of the court. The defendant even makes his own appointment for the initial interrogation, and there is no penalty for disregarding a subsequent summons.' These adjustments ensure that K is alone in his total responsibility for his own case. The advocate explains to him that one of the aims of the court is 'to eliminate all defence, the accused man must be left to his own devices'. What is being tried, essentially, is K's life: tried for its worth, its significance. 'In ignorance of the actual accusation and even of any further charges arising from it one had to recall the most trivial actions and events of one's life, present them and review them from every angle.' The thought makes K feel despondent – and old. 'How depressing such a task was. It was perhaps a suitably puerile occupation to help a pensioner while away the long days.'

Zadie Smith is lucid on the moral isolation of Kafka's protagonists. 'The ethical individual in Kafka cannot rely on the world for his morality,' she writes. At the end of *The Trial*, K turns, briefly and futilely, to the church. The priest, temporarily *en rôle* as reader, interprets the parable of the doorkeeper for K, then goes on to interpret the interpretation. Finally K interjects:

> 'I don't agree with that opinion,' said K, shaking his head, 'for if you accept it you must believe everything the doorkeeper says is true. But that this is not possible, you yourself have shown in detail.' 'No,' said the priest, 'one does not have to believe everything is true, one only has to believe it is necessary.' 'Depressing thought,' K said. 'It makes the lie fundamental to world order.'
>
> K said this in conclusion, but it was not his final verdict. He was too tired to follow all the deductions that could be drawn from the story; they led him into unaccustomed

> trains of thought, removed from reality and more suitable for academic discussion among court officials.

K's life, his trial, the parable: all are subjected to never-ending and therefore unsuccessful interpretation. Life as an interminable Rubik's cube, a puzzle that can never be solved. The lie – the childish yardsticks we use to lend structure to our lives – is what permits us to exist in the world.

'Correct understanding of a matter and misunderstanding the same matter do not exclude each other entirely,' the priest tells K. Contradiction is the heart of Kafka. His narratives are absurd, illogical; they proclaim the world incomprehensible, and yet in doing so, they pin down that incomprehensibility with great precision. These conceptual fireworks are the reward for slogging through prose that is often far from pleasurable. At his literary best, though, Kafka is untouchable as a writer of our dreams, master of that impossible language all of us somehow speak.

Alexander Nurnberg

Dissecting the Beetle: Franz Kafka's Sense of Humour

Humor can be dissected, as a frog can, but the thing dies in the process and the innards are discouraging to any but the pure scientific mind.

– E B White

There is an old interpreters' joke (there turns out, when you look into it, to be a whole genre of interpreter jokes) about the time Konrad Adenauer visited the UN. Adenauer stood up to address the General Assembly, launched into his speech, and spoke for quite some time, growing increasingly impassioned in his delivery. But the delegates could hear nothing through their headsets. They looked around the hall at each other in confusion, frantically twiddled the knobs on their sound systems. A senior diplomat rushed up to the interpreters' booth, saw the assembled team sitting in total silence and shrieked 'Why aren't you translating?!'. One turned round, shrugged apologetically and explained: 'We can't – we're waiting for the verb.'

For German, as Mark Twain said, is a 'perplexing language', 'slipshod and systemless, and so slippery and elusive to the grasp'. Clauses can build interminably upon clauses, and when they do, the grammatical principle of *satzklammer* means the verb is sent to the end of the sentence, leaving a reader or listener potentially unaware of its meaning until the very last word. Franz Kafka made able use of this linguistic built-in punchline. It is preserved in miniature form in the famous opening to *The Metamorphosis*:

> Als Gregor Samsa eines Morgens aus unruhigen Träumen

> erwachte, fand er sich in seinem Bett zu einem ungeheuer-
> en Ungeziefer verwandelt.

In German, the sentence itself mimics Gregor's dozy awakening. It opens slowly and prosaically, its mind still on the dreams of the night just passed, and it stretches out serenely until the arrival of the adjective – *ungeheueren*, huge – signals something unexpected. The noun that follows is a surprise: a generalised sort of vermin, an *Ungeziefer*, has made its way into this bedroom. But the verb, when it comes, is a shock. Only now do we realise that what Gregor has done to this insect – *verwandelt* – is turn into it.

There is something about that joke and this sentence that encapsulates the experience of reading Kafka. The text can feel impenetrable, like the worlds his characters tend to inhabit: labyrinthine cities and structures made up of endless corridors and staircases, rooms opening on to other rooms, systems of authority with uncountable layers. And as in the sentence above, the punchline, when it eventually arrives, may bring fresh bewilderment, not resolution. To read Kafka may make you feel like that audience at the UN, or as Mark Twain said he felt when he read anything in German: 'one is washed about in it, hither and thither, in the most helpless way.'

Perhaps for this reason, Kafka seems not to get much credit for his humour. The Merriam-Webster dictionary defines the adjective to which he has bequeathed his name as meaning '*especially:* having a nightmarishly complex, bizarre, or illogical quality' (the OED, sensibly, is more generic), but makes no mention of a comic one. And admittedly, the confusing worlds of Kafka's stories are regularly nightmarish, and tragic too. The story Kafka felt turned him into a true writer, which he completed in one night of frenzied work – 'The Judgment' – ends with its hero humiliated by his father and throwing himself off a bridge to his death. But contemporary accounts describe Kafka giggling uncontrollably as he read his work out to friends, and even the most solemn of readers could not fail to glimpse the occasional flash of comedy among the misfortune, like laughter in the dark. 'In the Penal Colony', whose plot may be the grimmest in all Kafka's stories, tells the tale of a society that sentences men to death without trial, and the gruesome execution machine that delivers it by engraving into its victims' skin, with torturous slowness, the words of the judgment passed down on them. No laughing matter, you would think – except that the officious bureaucrat administering the machine is so pompous in his grand explanations of the device, so clown-like, sweating in the sun in his thick winter uniform with two handkerchiefs tucked under the collar, so cartoonish in his frenetic tinkering at the controls, his constant complaints at the difficulty of obtaining spare parts for the horrific instruments within, that you find yourself chuckling guiltily and willing the action onward. You balk at the word, but it is *funny*. And despite E B White's warning about the likely consequences of explaining a joke, Kafka's humour deserves exploration, because it is not just an occasional bonus or distant echo in his work but a crucial facet of his art.

The caricatured bureaucrat in 'In the Penal Colony', together with his many half-relatives throughout Kafka's stories, should probably bear a lot of the blame for his author's sober reputation. In his introduction to the complete works, John Updike credited Kafka with great powers of foresight, pointing to the climates of guilt and fear and the vast systems of meaningless bureaucratic authority in his works and seeing them, as many readers have, as reminiscent (or more accurately, pre-cognisant) of the totalitarian politics of the Twentieth Century:

> Kafka's reputation has been immeasurably enhanced by his seeming prophecy, in works so private and eccentric, of the atrocious regimes of Hitler and Stalin, with their mad assignments of guilt and farcical trials and institutionalised paranoia. But the seeds of such vast evil were present in the world of the Emperor Franz Josef, and Kafka was, we should not forget, a man of the world, for all his debilities. He attended the harsh German schools of Prague; he earned the degree of Doctor of Law; he had experience of merchandising through his father's business. [...] Out of his experience of paternal tyranny and decadent bureaucracy he projected nightmares that proved prophetic.

The Trial makes this connection most explicit. Josef K wakes one morning to find that he is being arrested in response to an accusation that he cannot even determine, let alone defend. The low-level functionaries and ancillary characters he encounters either refuse to name the supposed crime, or else are so far removed from the distant echelons of power that they are unable to advise on its mysterious workings. Like any show-trial, the outcome is tragic: K is eventually sentenced to death, no less ignorant of his offence. The atmosphere throughout is oppressive. The action takes place in a weirdly circular city where buildings at one end of town connect impossibly to those on the other, where law courts are hosted in crowded attic rooms, and where the air itself is stifling and thick:

> The fuggy atmosphere in the room was unbearable, it actually prevented one from seeing to the other end[...] He peered from beneath his hand to see what was happening, for the reek of the room and the dim light together made a whitish dazzle of fog.
>
> 'You feel a little dizzy, don't you?' she asked [...] Don't worry,' she said. 'That's nothing out of the common here, almost everybody has an attack of that kind the first time they come here [...] the air, well, on days where there's a great number of clients to be attended to, and that's almost every day, it's hardly breathable.'

Wherever he goes, it seems, K searches desperately for doors, windows or skylights that he might open, but they are either blocked off, sealed shut or, if they are opened, no relief whatsoever:

> It was difficult to open, he had to push the latch with both hands. Then there came into the room through the great window a blend of fog and smoke, filling it with a faint smell of burning soot. Some snowflakes fluttered in too. 'An awful autumn,' came the voice of the manufacturer behind K.

This is nightmarish, certainly, and frighteningly so. But it is not an invention of the Twentieth Century. This is Dickens, describing the law courts of *Bleak House*:

> Well may the court be dim, with wasting candles here and there; well may the fog hang heavy in it, as if it would never get out; well may the stained-glass windows lose their colour and admit no light of day into the place; well may the uninitiated from the streets, who peep in through the glass panes in the door, be deterred from entrance by its owlish aspect and by the drawl, languidly echoing to the roof from the padded dais where the Lord High Chancellor looks into the lantern that has no light in it and where the attendant wigs are all stuck in a fog-bank! This is the Court of Chancery...

The word 'fog' appears 24 times in the first chapter of *Bleak House* alone, and throughout the novel the murk and mud are ubiquitous metaphors for the impenetrability of the judicial system – and the dirtiness of it. Like K in *The Trial*, 'scores of persons have deliriously found themselves made parties in Jarndyce and Jarndyce without knowing how or why'. You might argue that Dickens's tone is overtly comic, and the direction in Kafka more tragic – after all, Jarndyce and Jarndyce is a lawsuit about who will inherit a vast sum of money, while K's trial is a matter of life and death – but Dickens continually reveals that the iniquities of the system, with its slowness and meaningless impositions of power, drive many who encounter it to madness or the grave.

The totalitarian system and foggy atmosphere of *The Trial*, then, are nothing new. In fact Dickens, writing in a period 60 years before Kafka's, seems far more motivated by desire to expose its injustices. Kafka's innovation is his unblinking focus not on the system but on the individual and his psychological experience of it, on how it feels to face a world so vast and incomprehensible and so apparently capricious in its deeds. In this respect the judicial labyrinth of *The Trial*, though bleak, is just one of many metaphors for the disorienting world, like the snow-covered town in *The Castle*, with its winding, innavigable streets, or the incomprehensibly huge new country of *Amerika* – on whose shores the novel's hero, young Karl Rossman, has not even set his feet before he loses himself in the huge structure ('down endless recurring stairs, through corridors with countless turnings') of the ship that is taking him to it. This world is comically, farcically large. A tour of Karl's uncle's business in America reveals a building 'which took several days to traverse in its entirety, even if one did nothing more than have a look at each department'; the office in which the whole business once operated is now 'the restaurant and storeroom for the sixty-fifth group of porters'. Faced with such bewildering scale, a system of authority that hides some of its workings from view may even be doing so with benevolent aims. In this way, in 'The Great Wall of China', the wall is built piecemeal, in thousand-yard sections, and each architect is sent far away when their section is completed to start work on another – thereby saving them from the despair of knowing that the work will never be finished in their lifetimes. The fact that this means the great wall is built with gaps everywhere, and is therefore pointless, is just more reason to protect the workers from the truth.

Though the humour in Kafka often lies in the absurdities of these surreal situations, much is also delivered at the expense of his heroes – naïve, hopeless men of inaction who seem determined to be complicit in their demise. An early story, 'Wedding Preparations in the Country', tells of a man leaving town on his way to his fiancée's small village and of his constant nervous prevarication, his fretting over whether to have stayed longer in town, whether anybody will be there to collect him, whether the locals will make him go on boring walks, whether his friends will think his new wife is pretty, and so on. The story was never finished, and trails off in the middle of a sentence, but as such achieves a kind of artistic perfection – this hero was never going to make it to his wedding. In 'The Judgment', the poor suicide victim spends the first half of his story agonising over how much and what kind of news to send to his good friend who lives abroad, only to learn that his more decisive father has intervened and shared it already. In their anxious internal monologues these characters talk themselves into arguments more circular and contorted than any of the external systems to which they are subject. Faced with a godless, existentialist world they respond, like Vladimir and Estragon, by waiting for the verb, and can prefer even a malicious instruction to the uncertainty of having to make up their own minds. In *The Trial*, K briefly considers taking flight but instead waits patiently until he is called by the Inspector:

> The command itself was actually welcome to him. 'At last,' he shouted back, closing the cupboard and hurrying *at once* into the next room. [my italics]

K, like most of Kafka's characters, simply waits for 'that certainty which the natural course of things would be bound to bring'.

If they do act, these men usually do so only in reaction, asserting themselves in opposition to external circumstances and often causing themselves far greater problems as a result. When K is first arrested in *The Trial*, he remembers that a friend of his is a lawyer, and asks permission to telephone him. But when the Inspector says yes, K petulantly refuses, unwilling to continue on a course of action that has received the blessing of his captors – 'No, I don't want to now,' he says, like an outmanoeuvered child. But it is not just that these characters tend hilariously to make their lives more difficult: there is sometimes even a sense that they might be enjoying their misfortune. When K is distracted, in *The Castle*, by the charms of an alluring barmaid (demonstrating a weakness shared by his counterparts throughout these books), his experience of sleeping with her is oddly reminiscent of the general experience of reading Kafka:

> There, hours went past, hours in which they breathed as

> one, hours in which K was haunted by the feeling that he was losing himself or wandering into a strange country, farther than ever man had wandered before, a country so strange that not even the air had anything in common with his native air, where one might die of strangeness, and yet whose enchantment was such that one could only go on and lose oneself further.

This is no victim of external circumstance – however 'haunted' K may feel by this unfathomable new world. The comedy here is crucial, because it brings a light into the gloom of K's misfortune, shows agency and free will in a land that seemed impossibly constricting. With deliberate irony, Kafka demonstrates with his characters' very flaws – their inaction, their haplessness – the possibilities of self-determination, the path out of the maze. These novels would be 'a fine setting for a fit of despair,' as K realises in a moment of self-awareness in *The Castle*, 'if I were only standing here by accident instead of design'.

The humour, then, lies in the gap between the protagonists' understanding and the reality of their worlds. And they can be hopelessly uninformed about that reality. Like so much in Kafka, this thread begins in 'The Judgment', when the young hero Georg fails completely to understand that his father retains a mind of his own and, devastatingly, the strength to act on it. When the father asserts himself, Georg thinks at first he is joking – 'You comedian!', he shrieks nervously – but the joke is sadly on him. Its finest realisation is *The Metamorphosis*, where Georg has turned into Gregor but outgrown none of his predecessor's naivety. The literary purpose of the transformation – the reason Kafka made Gregor wake up in the form of a bug – is to dramatise the division between his mind and the world around him. It separates Gregor's mental state (in which he is confused, concerned and profoundly human) from the physical world (in which he is an insect), and in so doing reveals his utter failure to comprehend the external reality. When Gregor first wakes, transformed, he takes stock of his armour-plated back and segmented abdomen with sleepy concern and then reverts to worrying about his career. It is more than he can conceive. And in fact we never learn exactly what kind of creature he has become. Vladimir Nabokov, with his great loves of both entomology and close reading, was tempted to try to determine it and went to great lengths in his lectures on *The Metamorphosis* to identify the species, but the descriptions in Kafka's text are deliberately vague. The words *ungeheuren* and *Ungeziefer* are, as the translator Susan Bernofsky has pointed out, 'virtual non-entities', both words prefixed by un- and therefore essentially negative descriptors, defining what they are not. And in a now-famous letter to his first publishers, Kafka begged that they resist the urge to depict the insect on the cover – suggesting instead just an open doorway with a dark room beyond. The truth is that we should not know what creature Gregor has become, because he himself does not know, and with the narrative focused on his interior view we see him only through his own, now increasingly deteriorating eyes.

Gregor could be forgiven, as could anyone, for finding his metamorphosis incomprehensible – indeed its nightmarishness makes him a sympathetic man. But the purpose of his comic failures of percipience, like the metaphor of his weakening eyesight (or the Dickensian fog that follows K in *The Trial*), is to reveal the blindness that predated his transformation, the inability to recognise his position in the world. Gregor works to support his family and pay off his parents' debts: he believes he is shackled to his unpleasant, exhausting job for five or six years more at least. But his family, unbeknown to him, has built savings that would support them for as much as two years, and when Gregor's metamorphosis forces them to act, his father, mother and sister – supposedly too old, too asthmatic, and too ladylike respectively to work – all prove suddenly capable of earning for themselves. Gregor might have known he had more freedom, but 'of course he had not asked'. His naivety is often charming – like his secret grand ambition to sponsor his sister through the conservatoire, though we discover from the lodgers' response to her violin playing that there may be no talent to nurture there – but it is laughable too. Like all Kafka's heroes, Gregor makes you want to respond like the mysterious, parable-speaking priest in *The Trial:*

> And at that the priest shrieked from the pulpit: 'Can't you see anything at all?' It was an angry cry, but at the same time sounded like the involuntary shriek of one who sees another fall and is startled out of himself.

It is the hallmark of Kafka's writing that there is both tragedy and slapstick in the fall.

The same fissure, the same comic gap, lies in the language of these tales. Just as the protagonists perceive one version of reality, and the outside world offers back its quite different understanding, so the prose is limpid and patent where the situations it describes get ever murkier and more surreal. It delivers absurdity in a coolly matter-of-fact tone. For those of us who read Kafka in translation, it is impossible to know how much of this humour has been lost, but Thomas Mann spoke of Kafka's 'conscientious, curiously explicit, objective, clear and correct style, its precise, almost official conservatism', and much of this linguistic approach carries through. It is most overt in some of the short stories, where Kafka was toying with these extremes, as in this characteristic opening line:

> Honoured members of the Academy!
>
> You have done me the honour of inviting me to give your Academy an account of the life I formerly led as an ape.

But its subtler sounds reverberate throughout Kafka's work, constantly presenting its unexpected turnings, its impenetrable and impossible developments, in serious, incurious notes. It is the prose equivalent of the deadpan delivery.

And once more the comedy, while providing hilarious diversions, also serves a more profound purpose in the text. By presenting the absurd with a straight face, abstruse situations with clear-cut prose, Kafka dramatises for the reader the very bewilderment his protagonists feel. Po-faced and indisputable, he treats us in much the same way that his heroes are treated by the worlds they encounter. We perfectly understand their position. A similar stylistic effect is achieved through Kafka's use of detail: he and Max Brod were passionate disciples, according to Milan Kundera, of Flaubert, 'the master observer', and that influence is palpable in Kafka's approach. Even the most curious scenarios contain moments of sensitively witnessed, minutely realistic detail – often comic in themselves, like the officer in the penal colony trying to clean his bloodied hands first in dirty water, and then in sand – and these turn the impossible into the compellingly real, make the surreal suddenly plausible. In fact this is what most gives the stories their nightmarish quality: the vividness of the detail in these otherwise nebulous worlds. As readers, we share the experience of the protagonists, simultaneously baffled by reality and bound to it. The joke, therefore, is on all of us.

What this means is that though the fates suffered by these characters may be cruel, Kafka is not. Though he may mock his heroes' naivety, he forces his readers to recognise the same weakness in themselves, prompts us to share his affection. And throughout, in all the labyrinths, among the fog and the fear, he leaves clues that signal a way out. There is a parable in 'The Great Wall of China' about a message sent 'to you, the humble subject' by a dying emperor. The messenger sets out towards you, but has to struggle through the vast crowds around the bed, out through the palace and the throngs massed outside, the courts of the citadel and the walls around it and the fields beyond, on a journey so incomprehensibly far that it would take many thousands of years to accomplish, if ever it could be accomplished, and yet –

> But you sit at your window when evening falls and dream it to yourself.

And at the end of *The Trial*, when K is being led off by his guards for the final time, he comes to a realisation:

> 'The only thing I can do now,' he told himself, and the regular correspondence between his steps and the steps of the other two confirmed his thought, 'the only thing for me to go on doing is to keep my intelligence calm and discriminating to the end. I always wanted to snatch at the world with twenty hands, and not for a very laudable motive either. That was wrong, and am I to show that not even a whole year's struggling with my case has taught me anything? Am I to leave this world as a man who shies away from all conclusions? [...] I don't want that to be said.'

The external world, for all its complexity and power, is no match for the cogent mind. This is the lesson of Kafka's comedy. By dramatising the gap between his heroes' perceptions and the world around them, he promotes, above all, the individual mind, affirms its ability to determine its own conclusions, its potential to interpret reality.

He shows us that what we need to do, when faced with a bewildering world, is not to wait for the verb, but to choose it.

Alexander Nurnberg works for Google.

Adam Foulds

Kafka's 'The Burrow'

> Sometimes I heard the foxes as they ranged over the snow-crust, in moonlight nights, in search of a partridge or other game, barking raggedly and demoniacally like forest dogs, as if labouring with some anxiety, or seeking expression, struggling for light ... They seemed to be rudimental, burrowing men, still standing on their defence, awaiting their transformation. Sometimes one came near to my window, attracted by my light, barked a vulpine curse at me, and then retreated.

This is Henry David Thoreau in the 'Winter Animals' chapter of *Walden* imagining anxious, half-animal burrowing men and in so doing whimsically, unwittingly constructing a bridge between that work and the world of Kafka's 'The Burrow'. He thereby allows us to add his name to Borges's list of Kafka's precursors, a literary tradition retrospectively realigned by his individual talent. I seriously propose this addition to Borges's honour roll because, if the hint here is taken and the analogy pursued, it turns out that 'The Burrow' and *Walden* have a good deal in common. They are both chronicles of a period of time devoted to constructing, building, dwelling, gathering, of sensing the environment and thinking. They are preoccupied with solitude and neighbours, with food and shelter – and investigating what is really, ultimately true. The fact that their juxtaposition is at first surprising strikes me as proof of Emerson's idea that 'our moods do not believe in each other'. On the surface, *Walden* is so ruddy with healthy, clearheaded independence and productive physical work, while 'The Burrow' is so very much not, so full instead of the labours of anxiety, fruitless repetitions and darkness. But surfaces and what lies beneath them are complicated matters in both works and the following remarks will, I believe, reveal similarities at least as profound as the differences, similarities often disguised as differences, the two sides of one coin. Dwelling on the comparison will also, I hope, free me from the fear that besets anyone writing about Kafka that it has all been said before somewhere along the many shelves of Kafka criticism[1] but it probably cannot free me from the fear that pretty much all writing about Kafka is anyway beside the point. To pull open Kafka's stories, to take the material that Kafka so fastidiously stripped of its immediate connotations to get to the dense, glowing, radioactive dreamstuff of inner experience, and to reconnect them with ordinary rational thoughts and meanings is to play an endless and unlosable game of interpretation that is also unwinnable. It's all about kabbalah. It's all about anti-Semitism. It's all Freud. It's a critique of atomised urban life. And so on and so on.

1. UNDERGROUND / OVERGROUND

Kafka's title, *Der Bau*, is ambiguous for German readers, invoking a building as much as it does a burrow. It is used to refer to any kind of structure or construction. The burrow is a burrow and a building. This ambiguity is a corollary of that around the human or animal status of the narrator. The narrator talks (and talks) and thinks like a human, despite being an animal. The Animal is an animal and a person.

We can take these two things together and take them personally – 'The Burrow' is a person talking about a home. A person like Thoreau for whom burrowing and building are also linked, historically:

> We may imagine a time when in the infancy of the human race, some enterprising mortal crept into a hollow in a rock for shelter.

And now,

> Under the most splendid house in the city is still to be found the cellar ... The house is still but a sort of porch at the entrance of a burrow.

[1] Of course I don't know for a fact that this hasn't already been said. Perhaps I'm the fourth person to make the comparison, perhaps the ninth or the nineteenth.

This burrowing or building has particular dangers.

> If one designs to construct a dwelling-house, it behooves [the builder] to exercise a little Yankee shrewdness, lest after all he find himself in a workhouse, a labyrinth without a clue, an almshouse, a prison, or a splendid mausoleum instead.

It becomes clear in moments like this that *Walden*'s determined hopefulness is asserted in partial victory over the same fears that endlessly destroy the repose of Kafka's Animal, that Thoreau's fear is that he could become the animal, in a labyrinth without a clue. The project of *Walden* is to try to construct a dwelling and live while avoiding that danger. Obversely, it reminds us that all that's wrong with the Animal is its lack of Yankee shrewdness. Nothing ever actually goes wrong for the Animal. It is never attacked while it builds its labyrinth, prison, potential mausoleum.

2. INSIDE / OUTSIDE

One of the great jokes of 'The Burrow' (there are several) is that in order to assure itself that its underground fortress is secure and that it is truly safe inside, the Animal goes outside for a considerable time. There it experiences an expansive and healthy outdoor life:

> I am no longer confined by narrow passages, but hunt through the open woods, and feel new powers awakening in my body for which there was no room, as it were, in the burrow.

Note that 'as it were'. It's a grace note of the dominant themes: doubt, supposition, the constant revision of thought as it's uttered, the collapsing together of possibility and fact, and the dim recognition that everything would be alright if only the Animal could let it be. There is only no room down there 'as it were'. In reality there is plenty of room.

There is good hunting above ground and the chance to confront its fears, the spectres of the night 'in actuality with the calm judgment of the fully awake. And strangely enough I discover that my situation is not so bad as I had often thought, and will probably think again when I return to my house'. Momentarily, the Animal gets a grip on reality and has peace, the sleep that is normally functioning reason, until the questions start again.

> Dare I estimate the danger which I run inside the burrow from observations which I make when outside? Can my enemies, to begin with, have any proper awareness of me if I am not in my burrow? ... No, I do not watch over my sleep, as I imagined; rather it is I who sleep, while the destroyer watches.

In *Walden*, being outside is an easy source of joy. When he cleans his cabin, Thoreau delights in taking the contents of his burrow outdoors.

> It was worth the while to see the sun shine on these things and hear the free wind blow on them.

At Walden, outside is Nature, active, lustrous, full of purpose, innocent. It thrills Thoreau and fulfils him. Contact with it is at the heart of the project of *Walden*. 'I rejoice that there are owls,' 'No yard! but unfenced nature reaching up to your very sills,' etc.

I suppose I should acknowledge at this point that one of the main differences between the two texts is that Walden is a real place and the Burrow isn't. There is no Nature in Kafka, no living ecosystems, only a bestiary of (half-human) avatars – dogs, mice, cockroaches, apes, moles, jackals. They dwell mostly in human spaces, either verminously or as institutional subjects. The Animal of 'The Burrow' is unusual in this respect, inhabiting its own construction, what biologists would call its extended phenotype, although scientific language does nothing to illuminate this dark structure created by an unspecified, highly verbal[2] crea-

2. A better generic description might be found in Kierkegaard's 'The Seducer's Diary,' a text Kafka certainly knew:

> A person who goes astray inwardly has less room for manoeuvre; he soon finds he is going round in a circle from which he cannot escape ... I can imagine nothing more agonising than an intriguing mind which has lost the thread and then turns all its wits upon itself ... It is to no avail that he has many exits from his fox's earth; the moment his anxious soul thinks it sees daylight appearing, it proves to be a new entrance, and like startled game, pursued by despair, he is thus constantly seeking an exit and forever finding an entrance through which he returns into himself.

ture. It is a self-portrait in excavation, apparently modelled on memories of medieval fortresses. It is rambling, insecure, a kind of thinking to get lost in, riddled with pests and half-trashed by its owner.

With no further reassurance available or accepted from the outside world, the Animal retreats, with difficulty, into its inner space. Unlike for Thoreau, who invites the wilderness up to his window-sills and handily takes his furniture out into the free wind, transitioning between inside and outside is very difficult for the Animal. Exit is achieved after much thought, thought which is finally given up.

> ... is it not a dangerous, a far too dangerous stake that you are playing for? Can there be any reasonable grounds for such a step? No, for such acts as these there can be no reasonable grounds. But all the same, I then cautiously raise the trap door and slip outside...and fly as fast as I can from the treacherous spot.

The Animal can only re-enter when it has reached such a degree of exhaustion that again thought is overcome. But once back inside, the Animal experiences, momentarily, a kind of Waldenesque idyll, a present moment filled with purpose:

> ... inside the burrow I always have endless time – for everything I do there is good and important and satisfies me somehow.

For a moment, the Animal is Thoreau smiling in his bean field.

Of course, this doesn't last. Shortly afterwards the Animal hears the inlocatable whistling noise that will torment him for the rest of his narration and possibly the remainder of its life.[3] Anxiety is constant. The Animal's inner pastoral shrinks further into a closed central space, the Castle Keep, the silence of which the Animal now contemplates from an adjoining tunnel. Peace now only exists in an innermost inside, a holy of holies, that the Animal would destroy if it were entered. This is not, one suspects, an Animal that would trust any club that would have him as a member.

3. To play the unlosable, unwinnable game for a moment, imagine that the source of the ceaseless whistling sound is a tubercular lung.

3. BURROWING / THINKING

> While all the rest of the burrow is the outcome rather of intense intellectual than physical labour, the Castle Keep was fashioned by the most arduous labour of my whole body… But for such tasks the only tool I possess is my forehead. So I had to run with my forehead thousands and thousands of times, for whole days and nights, against the ground, and I was glad when the blood came, for that was a proof that the walls were beginning to harden…

Thinking and burrowing are activities that are continuous with each other, extensions of each other. Both texts collapse these ideas together, merge them, just as building above and below ground are merged. As the Animal suggests, rather strangely, some tunnels are the outcome of intellectual activity only; others need physical force.

Thoreau would like to tunnel with his head as well.

> I do not wish to be any more busy with my hands than is necessary. My head is hands and feet. I feel all my best faculties concentrated in it. My instinct tells me that my head is an organ for burrowing, as some creatures use their snout and fore paws, and with it I would mine and burrow my way through these hills.

In these two passages[4], vehicle and tenor elide, interchange. Thinking and tunnelling are equally metaphors for each other. They are figured as the same thing. But what is this thinking, this tunnelling, for?

4. DWELLING / KNOWING

First of all, the burrowing is to create a habitable place. After that comes the attempt to know, to 'investigate,' (to use one of the Animal's words), an effort to get to the bottom of things. For both Thoreau and the Animal, this is an existential matter. The Animal wants to be sure it's not about to be eaten. It wants to live. Thoreau wants to lead a life worth living.

Here's Thoreau in *Walden* sounding a lot like the Kafka of the letters

[4] *Passages.*

and diaries:

> I wanted to live deeply and suck out all the marrow of life ... to put to rout all that was not life, to cut a broad swath and shave close, to drive life into a corner, and reduce it to its lowest terms, and, if it proved to be mean, why then to get the whole and genuine meanness of it, and publish its meanness to the world; or if it were sublime, to know it by experience, and be able to give a true account of it in my next excursion.

Walden is a place to live 'deliberately,' to work out what is necessary for a life and to get to the facts of experience, burrowing down 'through New York and Boston and Concord, through Church and State, through poetry and philosophy and religion, till we come to a hard bottom and rocks in place, which we can call *reality*, and say, This is, and no mistake'.

The Animal's investigations are apparently for less philosophical ends. All he wants to know is where the whistling sound comes from, whether it comes from a beast and therefore presages a violent death. But unlike Thoreau, the Animal cannot establish any facts. (Here again, inhabiting an inexhaustible metaphor rather than a real place probably doesn't help). The Animal can generate out of its fear endless unstable facts, facts with a short half-life, constantly degrading, constantly replaced by others. One of the fascinations of the story is watching this process of imagined possibilities solidifying with fear and becoming actualities:

> I can explain the whistling only in this way: that the beast's chief means of burrowing is not its claws, which it probably employs as a secondary resource, but its snout or its muzzle, which, of course, apart from its enormous strength, must also be fairly sharp at the point... This indrawal of breath, which must be an earthshaking noise, not only because of the beast's strength, but of its haste ... this noise I hear then as a faint whistling. But quite incomprehensible remains...

Probably. Of course. Must be. Because of. I hear then. All this about a beast that in all likelihood does not exist, of which there is certainly no real proof. Still, the investigation has to be undertaken with this frantic tunnelling, from first principles, from whatever evidence can be adduced, because, as for the stoutly empirical Thoreau at Walden burrowing down below Concord and philosophy, in the Animal's words, 'one is not at liberty to make a priori assumptions'. The Animal is as committed as Thoreau to a final reckoning with reality whether it prove comforting or 'mean':

> ...truth will bring me either peace or despair, but whether the one or the other, it will be beyond doubt or question.

Interestingly, in both 'The Burrow' and *Walden*, this activity of thinking and verification is imagined as a state of being beside oneself, solitary but double, in calm self-surveillance, the Animal guarding its own burrow. Here's Thoreau:

> With thinking we may be beside ourselves in a sane sense. By a conscious effort of the mind we can stand aloof from actions and their consequences; and all things, good and bad, go by us like a torrent.

But for the Animal this experience is all too fleeting. As it loses faith in the value of the observations made from outside the burrow, it realises that it is not watching over its sleep. It becomes one frightened, lonely, limited animal again. It is instead the unseen destroyer that has the prerogative of watching over things.

For Thoreau, the establishing of a fact is a thrillingly violent event, almost orgasmic, a *petit mort*, a consummation.

> If you stand right facing and face to face to a fact, you will see the sun glimmer on both its surfaces, as if it were a cimeter, and feel its sweet edge dividing you through the heart and marrow, and so will happily conclude your mortal career.

But the Animal is always totalising possibilities into facts that won't hold still and stay true or be proven. Endless blades swish down over the huddled and terrified creature and vanish before they strike. The Animal cannot conclude its mortal career.

5. TIME AND TERMINUS

Walden and 'The Burrow' are both chronicles of a period of time in their author's lives. That time is linear and seasonal. 'When autumn sets in,' opines the Animal, 'to possess a burrow like mine and a roof over your head, is great good fortune for anyone getting on in years.' Thoreau recounts his seasons, winter and spring. *Walden* tells of the events of a year.

> This was my first year's life in the woods completed; and the second year was similar to it. I finally left Walden September 6th, 1847.

But in both works another kind of experiential time is active. In *Walden* it supervenes in moments of meditative absorption in the present. In 'The Burrow' it is a present tense that disrupts and destabilises the time scheme of the narration, a product of the Animal's anxiety, its confusion, revision and lack of conclusions.

Thoreau quotes Confucius and the *Bhagavad Gita* through his book and declares that he wishes to 'stand on the meeting of two eternities, the past and future, which is precisely the present moment; to toe that line'. To be fully present in the now is to live in and beyond time simultaneously, in the manner of the Daoists or Zen masters:

> Time is but the stream I go a-fishing in. I drink at it; but while I drink I see the sandy bottom and detect how shallow it is. Its thin current slides away but eternity remains.

Be that as it may, these experiences have linear durations and take place within calendrical time. When Thoreau has had enough of them at Walden, he leaves, on the date given above.

If the Animal had a calendar, it would seem that it could mark the day of the opening sentence of the story: 'I have completed the construction of my burrow and it seems to be successful.' But this temporal security, like all of the Animal's facts, does not last. The present moment of the story, the point of completion of the burrow, becomes increasingly difficult to locate, as the history of its construction, maintenance and alteration, as well as the Animal's thoughts and habits, are narrated in an urgent historical present that threatens to overwhelm the chronicle.

> True, the two entrances would double the risk, but that consideration need not delay me, for one of the entrances, serving merely as a post of observation, could be quite narrow. And with that I lose myself in a maze of technical speculations, I begin once more to dream my dream of a completely perfect home and that somewhat calms me.

When is the Animal calmed? Is it in the absolute now of the chronicle or in the period when the Animal is outside the burrow? It seems to be the latter. Repeatedly, the reader can, with effort, establish when things have happened in relation to some if not all of the other things, but then one loses one's footing again as an unfixable present tense floods into the chronicling, overwhelming clear sequence. Later, when the whistling starts, the problem gets worse.

> …that beautiful dream is past and I must set to work…

So the burrow is not completed? But when did the Animal think it was – where exactly between the beginning of the narrated events and the start of the whistling is the beginning of the story? It doesn't matter. The Animal's activity, sensory, excavatory and ratiocinative, is endless and without issue. 'The Burrow' is one of the last things that Kafka wrote and was never prepared for publication. It seems that an ending for the story was discarded. As it comes down to us, the story finishes in a moment of stasis, a hollow between waves of anxiety:

> …if it heard me I must have noticed some sign of it, the beast must at least have stopped its work every now and then to listen. But all remained unchanged.

In a moment, we have no doubt, the Animal will continue toiling at its defences, thinking them through in a world without facts or conclusions, dreaming of the end.

> Sometimes I dream that I have reconstructed it, transformed it completely, quickly, in a night, with a giant's

> strength, nobody having noticed, and now it is impregnable; the night in which such dreams come to me are the sweetest I know, tears of joy and deliverance still glisten on my beard when I awaken.

What a happy animal the Animal would have been in such circumstances, what a sturdy and proficient homesteader. Then it could have crossed the bridge back the other way into Walden, a world that is as similar to, as different from its own as a mirror image.

Adam Foulds's latest novel, *In the Wolf's Mouth*, is out now.

Costa Prize Winner 2009
Forward Prize Shortlist
T S Eliot Prize Shortlist

Lucinda Gane, Christopher Reid's wife, died in October 2005. *A Scattering* is his tribute to her and consists of four poetic sequences, the first written during her final illness, and the other three at intervals after her death.

Christopher Reid received the Somerset Maugham Award and the Hawthornden Prize for his first collection, *Arcadia*, and the 2000 Signal Poetry Award for his children's collection. He has twice been nominated for the Whitbread Awards. His *Letters of Ted Hughes* appeared in 2007, and his Selected Poems were published by Faber in November 2011.

'A beautiful book... [that] performs the miracle of bringing the dead back to life.'

– Adam Newey, *Guardian Review*

'Heartbreaking... [they] exemplify the best of what Areté has published'

– Lachlan Mackinnon, *Guardian*

'A life-affirming collection, full of urgency and feeling.'

– 2009 Costa Poetry Prize Judges

£7.99 paperback
ISBN: 978-0-9554553-6-0
Available from:
Areté,
8 New College Lane
Oxford
OX1 3BN
Online: www.aretemagazine.com

For further information please contact Claire Lowdon on 01865 289193, or email aretebooks@gmail.com

Roger Lewis

Kafka: Difficulties with Girls

'I passed the brothel as if it were the house of the beloved.'

– Franz Kafka.

My friend Willie Donaldson was said to have died from respiratory ailments brought on by crack cocaine. Quite possibly. But when the police broke down the door of his flat at 139 Elm Park Mansions, on 22 June 2005, they discovered, in addition to the corpse, a computer still logged on to a lesbian porn channel. So it is also feasible that Willie (the genius behind the Henry Root letters) died wanking – if not of wanking.

It could happen to the best of us. My own handmaiden of choice calls herself Pinky June. 'I like wearing pink and I like experimenting with girls.' The actress is also dependably very kind to pizza delivery boys and chaps who help show her the ropes in the gym.

Her party trick is to smoke a cigarette in a very unusual way – the viewer marvels at her flexibility and pulsations, as well as having to concur that Pinky at least won't get lung cancer in a hurry, inhaling in that fashion.

Most porn stars look foolish. The camera zooms in and it could be a gynaecology seminar. The flash and quiver of Pinky June's bare shoulders and the crenulations left by her elasticised waist straps would divert even Clare Quilty, who'd otherwise find her too unpubertal and ripe. Pinky June is pretty, young and slender and obliging – a happy huntress. But from some angles her face is almost ugly, sullen and pulpy. Her real name is Annely Gerritsen, she is five-foot four, weighs 45 kilograms, measures 32-23-34, and was born, an Aquarian, in Prague. I am not sure, however, that I want it confirmed that she exists in the real world, the place characterised by Willie Donaldson in his novel *Is This Allowed?* as containing the objective truth of 'weddings in Hampshire, dry-cleaning and money off, DIY and Final Demands, guttering and veins'. Pinky's sensual magic can remain on the screen. With her Czech credentials, she is of course the cunning little vixen, a dark-eyed lady from the forest, stalking and pouncing, a creature of instinct and naturalness. A fox.

The paradox of Pinky June is this: she does retain a sort of innocent purity.

To remain in the purlieus of Prague, it is sometimes said that 'Josefine the Singer' is an allegory about the Jews and Jewishness; oppression, persecution – the Jews as vermin, 'the mouse-people', a topos used by Art Spiegelman in *Maus*. Not a bit of it. Surely it is about sex – song as a barely concealed symbol of the orgasm?

'To understand her art,' says Kafka of Josefine, 'you need not just to hear her, but also to see her.' And what the crowd sees is a girl who can simultaneously be strikingly delicate or plain and crude. Others with similar skills or tastes, we are told, would 'surely have crept away in fear and shame' – but Josefine (like Pinky June) is triumphant because self-confident. Then there is the sexual trope of being watched, the breach of privacy: distractions, disruptions, disturbances off-stage only seem 'to heighten the effect of her singing'. Can singing be Kafka's actual subject? 'She is ready and waiting, the delicate creature, trembling alarmingly, especially below the breast. It is as if she had concentrated all her energy in her singing; as if everything in her that did not directly serve her singing had been drained of all her energies, almost of every possibility of life.' Her pose on the podium? 'Head flung back, mouth half-open, eyes raised aloft.' Think of Bernini's Saint Teresa and its famous fusion of spiritual and carnal ecstasy.

The way Josefine puckers her lips, 'exhales the air between her dainty front teeth, swoons in admiration at the sounds she herself is producing, and uses her dying fall to spur herself on to new feats, further and further beyond her own understanding', is precisely and uncannily a description of erotic play. As Molly Bloom whimpers, when similarly transported, yes I will yes I said yes.

'Spring,' said Janáček, of *The Cunning Little Vixen*, which was first performed in Brno in 1924, five months after Kafka's death, 'is in the forest, but also old age'. It is necessary to accept – to have sympathy with – our part in nature; passing the parcel to the next generation; the cycle of death and rebirth, no matter how exuberant or bursting with vitality we may feel. Pinky June, her website unamended, has remained eighteen years of age for several years now, and the pathos in Kafka's story is that Josefine grows old. She limps. Her coloratura falters. The public grows bored – they are no longer transfixed or interested. She is a former star in a pitiable state. 'She would love to sing, but simply cannot.' Yet once upon a time her admirers were intent, and intense, 'fervently listening, bodies packed close, hardly daring to breathe'. As Willie Donaldson, who went bankrupt with show business ventures twice, said, 'sex is the only department in life in which I have demanded from anyone taking part the very highest standards of seriousness'.

* * *

This is a theme of each of the stories making up *The Hunger Artist* quartet: that no matter how bizarre the speciality – aerial feats; disputation and illness; public displays of anorexia; singing / fucking – the protagonist is a yearning and solemn figure, capable of noble feelings. In 'First Sorrow', for example, we meet a disconsolate trapeze virtuoso, who conceals himself 'high in the music hall domes... He would remain night and day high up on the trapeze'. He is scarcely human – uncommunicative, solitary, like a watchful, disappointed bird. (Kafka / *kavka*: the jackdaw.) 'The management forgave him for this, because he was such an extraordinary, irreplaceable artist.' He 'maintained his art in all its perfection', so allowances are made. Allowances such as you'd make to a madman.

He finds touring increasingly irksome and impossible, for instance. He crouches (perches) fearfully on the luggage racks of railway carriages, and can't wait to be 'suspended once more from his trapeze on high'. Like an animal made miserable by being transplanted from its habitat – to a zoo or new home and alien environment – he finds that travel has a 'ruinous effect' on his nerves. He can never, in fact, be at peace – rehearsing his act obsessively; trying to better himself by leaping on to a second trapeze bar. Once he starts worrying about changing or developing his routines, his worries grow in intensity. How can he ever be calmed down? Only perhaps by death.

Similarly, in 'A Little Woman', once the narrator starts thinking and worrying and pondering and considering, there is no end to it. The story concerns two strangers, the male narrator and a woman who hates him without knowing him. It is a comedy about the tragic effects one person can have upon another (anonymous) person. The narrator denies a love affair but the story surely addresses, in wildly extreme form, the inevitable asymmetry of emotions between people. He feels nothing; her existence is ruined by his existence: 'I tried to point out to her how best to put an end to this constant vexation, but simply by doing so I put her into such an outburst of passion that I shan't attempt to repeat it again.' So they can't be complete strangers, then. Complete independence is impossible; absolute freedom unlikely. Other people impinge. They, the little woman and the narrator, are in a relationship. 'Every particle of my life would assuredly be a vexation to her', but masochistically this is what this woman wants, so it is what he provides – and a mad balance or fandango is achieved.

People torment each other simply by existing. Each hour is a trial – and the story is crammed with legal terminology and justifications. The narrator seeks a way of calling upon 'the ultimate court of appeal'. He is beset, as Oscar Wilde was in 1895, by mendacious witnesses, 'the most zealous of tell-tales'. The woman accusing him of causing her torment 'is a total stranger to me, and the relationship that exists between us has been contrived by her alone' – how often have we heard that line of defence in the Operation Yew Tree cross-examinations? The narrator is convinced the wider world 'will stick to her judgment and always decide against me... I shall not emerge from the proceedings undamaged'.

It is also an allegory of the artist and his audience, the artist and his model, the artist and his Muse (or inner voices): proximity and separation; endemic misunderstanding.

The punishments are psychological. In the title story, 'The Hunger Artist', ramifications are physical, and only afterwards psychological. Historically, Hunger Artists were to be found as part of circus sideshows, setting themselves up in 'booths in village fairs'. They were men who deliberately turned starvation into a spectator sport. In 1880, for example, Henry Tanner spent 40 days getting more and more emaciated in New York. Arthur Schnitzler, in 1896, saw Giovanni Succi grow thinner and thinner in Vienna. I suppose there is something extraordinary – if foolhardy – about people doing such extreme things to their body, sitting in a cage ('lit by torches, to heighten the effect'), seeing how long they can last without sustenance. Like a grand opera singer, actor-manager, or celebrity of any stamp, the hero of this tale is fussed over by impresarios, ostentatiously attended by doctors, an orchestra plays. For 40 days he refuses 'even the tiniest morsel'. Like Christ coming down from the cross, he has a prominent ribcage, protuberant bones. 'He placed his skeletal arms freely into the hands the young ladies stretched out.'

Yet as with the ageing singers, the public gets bored. Hunger artistry is as monotonous as dance marathons or long distance running. The hero of the story finds that people have drifted off, uninterested in 'this little bundle of bones'. If he starts raging, however, and flinging himself against the bars of his cage, it is not because he is unappreciated – it's because he has always been appreciated in the wrong way. He doesn't want his physical feat to have been a stunt. He wants it to be seen as having a spiritual dimension: 'there were no bounds to his capacity for hungering'. His 'dark temper of mind' is caused by his despair that no one ever quite took him seriously – he's the freak or record-breaker. What counts for him are the nobler aspirations, the spiritual aspects of extreme self-denial. The strict mortification of the flesh. (Kafka once saw Max Brod spread butter on a slice of bread and was nauseated. 'How *can* you swallow that fat? A lemon is the best food.')

* * *

So: a trapeze artist (a man literally in flight); a character seeking to escape 'a little woman' (a man figuratively in flight); a performance artist starving himself to death as a way of disappearing; a soprano who may also be a sexual athlete: the variety of life in Kafka's four tales, first published as *Ein Hungerkunstler* in 1924, represents a Dadaist music hall bill – a circus of horrors. I am reminded that W C Fields made a film called *The Man on the Flying Trapeze*, released in 1935, which has nothing to do with the circus – except the circus as metaphor; surviving, coping, managing; what a performance getting through the day is; the escalation of disasters and disappointment and misunderstanding. Fields is Ambrose Woolfinger, and there are burglars singing drunkenly in his cellar. 'We're in danger, I tell you,' frets his wife. 'We're in terrible danger, Ambrose.' Ambrose's reply is succinct: 'Maybe they mistook our cellar window for a stage door.' Later, he is arrested by a policeman in the street. 'Did I hurt you?' asks the cop disingenuously. 'How could you hurt anybody throwing them on their head?' Fields says, with only slight astonishment. The forces of law and order further enmesh him when the judge mistakes him for a criminal: 'Have you a permit to manufacture applejack?' – 'I guess

I could get one easy enough.' – 'Thirty dollars or thirty days. Take him away.' – 'But Judge...' – 'Clear the court! Clear the court!'

An intriguing thought: Kafka (b 1883) may have seen Fields (b 1880) in person in Vienna, Berlin, Paris or Leipzig. Heralded as 'America's Greatest Burlesque Juggler', Fields spent the years 1900 to 1904, 1909 to 1911, and 1913 to November 1914 touring around Continental theatres, 'Presenting a Repertoire of Comic and Difficult Tricks' – and *The Man on the Flying Trapeze*, like nothing else, represents the authentic Kafkaesque nightmare: involuntary confinement. Every book Kafka wrote is about confinement – in a building, a room, a body, a mind, in the demands of domesticity, or in an inextricable debate. We are each of us trapped by grammar and language (Czech and German in his case: 'I write differently to how I speak, and I speak differently to how I think, and so it continues, right to the deepest darkness'); by trying to understand each other in ways that are better than an approximation. We are trapped by physique – by physical states: feeding ourselves, maintaining ourselves, watching the body grow older, feebler. And in *The Hunger Artist* quartet, Kafka expresses his sheer bewilderment – even his outrage; loathing; astonishment – at the way we possess (or are possessed by) bodies. This theme is explored at length, obviously, in 'The Metamorphosis'. But whether it is the carapace of a cockroach, the translucent skin of Josefine's audience of mice, or the exoskeleton of castle dungeons and (as in Welles's film of *The Trial*) the unlit Gare d'Orsay, Kafka is the laureate of claustrophobia, of containment. He was also the professional expert in insurance claims, risk assessment and industrial accidents – burns, concussion, dismemberment, blinding and so forth. The artist and the insurance man both focus on the flesh. (He had a doctorate in it. On 18 July 1906, he was granted his degree in Jurisprudence at the Imperial and Royal Karl-Ferdinand German University in Prague and got a position with the Workers' Accident Insurance Institute for the Kingdom of Bohemia.)

Everywhere, his work seems deserted, and also crowded: ghostly throngs of (jeering) jurors; mute or catcalling congregations; or else there are piles of inert paper or straw. 'If we listen to the rapid pacing of someone, say at night, when everything about is quiet', he wrote in a haunting sentence in his notebook, 'we can hear the rattle of a loosely hung mirror against the wall.' People are hemmed in. Though they are squashed together, like tenants in a labyrinthine apartment building, Kafka's people are also, however, unable, or unwilling, to connect. His corridors seem to bear the sign: Standing Room Only. The artistes in *The Hunger Artist*, in particular, are solitaries, solipsists, egomaniacs: we become aware that their brains bustle to such an extent, there is (literally) no space (or time) to admit to or allow the reality of anyone else. It's almost as if they in fact enjoy being 'bleary-eyed, racked by headaches', as they ensure all is reasoned, contemplated, aforethought. If their bodies are deliberately buffeted, so is the brain tormented – but this is what the brain is for. Hemingway says as much in the chapter in *A Moveable Feast* entitled 'Hunger Was Good Discipline': the paintings in Parisian galleries 'were sharpened and clearer and more beautiful if you were belly-empty, hollow-hungry. I learned to understand Cezanne much better and to see truly how he made landscapes when I was hungry. I used to wonder if he were hungry too when he painted; but I thought possibly it was only that he had forgotten to eat'. Discriminations get finer and finer, disturbances sink deeper and deeper, until people become insane. Yet it is at the point of death that Kafka's characters sense they are most alive. Weak, they have huge strength: 'Anyone who can get quite so vexed,' he nevertheless says ironically, 'is probably quite able to get over the consequences of their vexation.'

The paradox made me think of Philip Larkin's mother, Eva, who spent her life as a whining invalid, the kind of woman who had to have a lie down after extreme exertions like doing the washing up. She lived to be 91. Eva discovered that considerable power and control can be found in remaining supine and dependant – for then everyone is at your beck and call. It was enough, anyway, to put Larkin off women for life. A letter to Kingsley Amis in 1943 gives his views: 'As far as I can see, all women are stupid beings. What is more, marriage seems a revolting institution, unless the parties have enough money to keep reasonably distant from each other... A lonely bachelorhood interspersed with buggery and strictly-monetary fornication seems to me preferable.' Two years later, he enlarges on his fears about being cramped in a letter to J B Sutton, a school friend from Coventry: 'It is a disturbing experience to have someone utterly dependent on you... One has no elbow room. I feel as if my wings were in danger of being clipped.'

Larkin, in a further letter to Sutton, tried to make his wishes above all to be alone seem noble – aesthetically lofty and necessary: 'I find that once I "give in" to another person... there is a slackening and dulling of the peculiar artistic fibres that make it impossible to achieve that mental 'clenching' that crystallises a pattern and keeps it still while you draw it... This letting-in of a second person spells death to perception... as well as the ability. Time and again I feel that before I write anything else at all I must... contemplate glittering loneliness. Marriage, of course... is impossible if one wants to do this.' What won't survive of him is love, because he never knew what love meant: 'I am a long way off being capable of any emotion as simple as what is called love. It seems limiting and man-eating to me.'

Larkin's phobia about commitment chimes with Jimmy Savile's. Savile had no oven in any of his flats because 'an oven means cooking and cooking means women and that means brain damage'. The ancestor of such morbid bachelordom is Kafka (not Sherlock Holmes – who was a homosexual), for whom women or wives were hateful shrews. This is 'A Little Woman': 'Day after day... I will leave the house enjoying the early morning, and I will see this face, bad-tempered because of me, the ill-humoured curl of the lip... the bitter smile painfully hollowing her prim little face, the plaintive heavenward glance.' His fear of 'that little woman's raging' was similar to Larkin's dread of having a wife who'd end up calling him a 'funny, silly creature' – and it is why Kafka could be engaged while remaining disengaged; betrothed but unmarried; and it is also why Welles structured his film of *The Trial* around Josef K's polite and frantic efforts to elude a succession of predatory females and temptresses: Jeanne Moreau, Elsa Martinelli, Romy Schneider, Suzanne Flon, Madeleine Robinson and Paola Mori. 'Even under the most favourable circumstances,' Kafka confided in his diary, 'it is probable that in a happy union I would despair. What I have to do, I can only do alone. Become clear about the ultimate things.' *Letters to Milena* (1920-1921, trans 1953) charts his disillusioned relationship with Milena Jesenska, the translator of his early prose. *Letters to Felice* (1912–1917, trans 1969) accounts for his courtship of Felice Bauer – another doomed attempt to face (and face up to) marriage. Larkin's *Letters to Monica* is fully in the tradition: a willing partner sadomasochistically led a dance. Here are male persons disinclined, metaphorically, ever to ejaculate inside someone else. (Welles's Josef K is Anthony Perkins – aka Norman Bates of *Psycho*.)

The meaning is that women are safer – nobler – in the mind than in actuality; than in the real contingent world of fears, scenes, doors slamming, harsh silences, pain, jealousy, and helplessness. Sex, Larkin complained to Jean Hartley, continuing the washing machine analogy, 'is so difficult. You ought to be able to get it and pay for it monthly like a laundry bill'. Which brings me neatly back to porn stars, who, when they have no clothes on, are splendid and unimprovable things 'to wank to, or with, or at', in Larkin's clear-headed and challenging epitome. They are direct and obvious and in every way alive.

So would Kaka, had he come across his fellow Czech in another existence, have been emboldened to write *Love Letters to Pinky June*? Would he be mesmerised? Disgusted? Fascinated? She'd have been ideal for him. And perhaps they did meet – if Pinky is a reincarnation of the mysterious and unknown girl described by Dora Geritt, whose 'Brief Memories of Franz Kafka' appears as Appendix IV in the 1947 edition (though not in any subsequent edition) of Brod's biography:

> In rustic retirement, amidst gentle hills and woods, amid winter's snow, Kafka was undergoing a rest-cure, which his failing health imposed on him, lying on the verandah of a little guest-house.
>
> He passed a lot of his time with a lively girl whose age it was hard to guess, who was obviously telling him a lot of interesting things of a general character, but never things about herself. Then one morning as she was coming up to his deck-chair, he greeted her with animation and said, 'I've been dreaming about you! Dressed in a wide, swelling, brown silk dress, hemmed with red hearts at the bottom, you were walking with long, swinging, elastic movements along a very broad, long road – and a tall, slim red-headed man came joyfully to meet you. You opened your arms and called out in a loud and relieved voice, "At last !" Tell me, have you ever had an experience like that in your life ?' She gave a quiet smile and said, 'Yes, plenty of men have taken an interest in me, but there was only one where I felt I had met my fate...'

The authentic note of difficulty and the indestructible dream of the perfect match.

The black panther replaces the Hunger Artist in his circus cage. Glory in the animal body replaces the self-destructive power of mind over matter: 'this noble body ... seemed to carry its freedom around with it ... Its joy of life came with such fiery breath from its jaws.'

Roger Lewis, who was recently awarded The Anthony Burgess Prize for Arts Journalism, is the author of biographies of Peter Sellers, Laurence Olivier, Charles Hawtrey and Anthony Burgess, and of the memoirs *Seasonal Suicide Notes* and *What Am I Still Doing Here ?* He is currently working on a book to be called *Growing Up With Comedians.*

TIGER COUNTRY
a play by Nina Raine

Tiger country is out of sight, out of mind, beyond the conscious and the rational. It is where animal instinct stirs and an irrefutable eye opens. Where we make contact with the unknown.

Tiger Country, Nina Raine's third play, is about the way we feel our way. About medicine as method acting. It is a hospital play that re-imagines and re-thinks territory annexed by the TV soaps.

'Raine is a huge talent'
– Libby Purves, *The Times*

23 October 2010
ISBN: 978-0-9562739-3-2
£7.99 paperback

Available from:
Areté,
8 New College Lane
Oxford
OX1 3BN

or: www.aretemagazine.com

'a witty, highly intelligent, PC-scourging sensibility… Raine writes with a fine mix of astringent objectivity and empathy'

– Paul Taylor, *Independent*

'I have seldom been so moved in the theatre'

– Paul Callan, *Daily Express*

'this play is replete with bold writing. Irreverent and unsentimental'

– Henry Hitchings, *Evening Standard*

'pacy, action-packed and, in places, touching… She is plainly a strong talent'

– Quentin Letts, *Daily Mail*

For further information please contact Claire Lowdon on 01865 289193, or email aretebooks@gmail.com

Oliver Reynolds

Metamorthingumajig

Lights up. Desk and chair. McGINTY *standing, besuited. Looks left.*

McGINTY: Yes.

Blackout. Lights up. EVANS *at desk in sweatshirt, sweatpants and trainers.* McGINTY *standing.*

EVANS: A man and a woman. Both staff. Both not well.

McGINTY: How so?

EVANS: Her hand giving her gyp. Him puking.

McGINTY: Location?

EVANS: The castle. Kitchen. Pan on the hob and pan on the floor. Both bubbling.

McGINTY: Both?

EVANS: Both.

McGINTY: Please continue your most interesting account.

EVANS: The cat scrammed

McGINTY: Scrammed?

EVANS: Scratched. The cat scratched Little Johnny.

McGINTY: Little Johnny.

EVANS: The same. The baby crying.

McGINTY: A baby? Where? Whose?

EVANS: In the crib. Not mine.

McGINTY: Whose then?

EVANS: Not mine.

The lights blink once. McGINTY *holds out a lidded glass jar.*

McGINTY: Do you recognise this?

EVANS: Pickle? Jam? Piccalilli?

McGINTY: What's in it.

EVANS: What's in it?

McGINTY: You don't recognise it?

EVANS: You can't recognise something you can't see.

McGINTY: Logic already.

EVANS: I can't see anything.

McGINTY: And now?

McGINTY holds the jar level with EVANS'*s eyes.*

McGINTY And now?

McGINTY holds the jar into his face.

EVANS: An aphid? [*āf'id*]

McGINTY: Aphid. [*af'id*] We had a call from the Hotel Hermann. The ninth floor was rank with them. The description of one guest – paying cash – not a country kilometre from your good self. Seems you'd been introducing them into the rooms.

EVANS: Introducing?

McGINTY: Keyholes. Windows. Under the doors.

EVANS: In jam-jars?

McGINTY: Wild.

EVANS: Ferocious.

The lights blink twice.

EVANS: I can see you keep limber. Toned. Tight. Just an observation. Tennis? Squash? An avid user of the courts, anyway. Or is it avid? [*ā'vid*] Just an observation. But don't you resent the self-assurance of the fit? Like this jogger who cut me up outside the paper-shop. Not that

I buy papers. Or read them. I was just passing. Cut me up on the pavement and accelerated away, self-assured buns joggling in concert.

McGINTY: Buns?

EVANS: Cheeks, then. Gluteus thingimus times two. My eyes, of course ditto. Joggling away. I hold my hands up. Only exercise I get.

The lights blink three times.

EVANS: You had a call from the Hotel Hermann?

McGINTY: A complaint.

EVANS: The complainant being

McGINTY: Not happy that his room was, one, infested and, two, that the infestation was unnatural.

EVANS: How so?

McGINTY: It was man-made.

EVANS: The man in question

McGINTY: Being yourself.

EVANS: Naturally.

McGINTY: The complainant says he recognised you.

EVANS: From what distance?

McGINTY: Excuse me?

EVANS: How far away was he when he made me? How dim were the night-lights?

McGINTY: Not on record.

EVANS: How can you make what you can't see?

McGINTY: Pardon?

EVANS: How can you make what you can't see?

McGINTY: Some details are skimpy.

EVANS: Thanks for that. Skimpy. What nationality was the complainant?

McGINTY: None.

EVANS: Pardon?

McGINTY: Stateless.

EVANS: A bug-eyed extra-terrestrial? Or an aphid? [*ā'fid*]

McGINTY: A Kurd.

EVANS: A Kurd. That's close enough.

The lights blink three times.

McGINTY: No-one wants you walking round in circles.

McGINTY *looks left. Blackout. Lights up.* EVANS *is now barefoot.*

McGINTY: No one wants you rudderless. But direct and to the point. Looking down at you from a great height – the hawk's-eye view – we want to see nothing but straight lines. Clarity. Beyond the flesh-and-blood some saving diagram. Think of the stick-man lighting the way to the emergency exit. Through the smoke and gloom. The murky corridors. Be our stick-man. Bare bones. Bare bones and a slack mouth.

The lights blink twice.

McGINTY: You're familiar with the Euler Bridge Problem.

EVANS: Not intimately.

McGINTY: You're in a city with a river, with bridges and recreational islands. One river, seven bridges and two islands, say. Let's say it's Prague.

EVANS: I'm not sure it is.

McGINTY: You said you don't know the problem.

EVANS: Not intimately.

McGINTY: Let us say Prague.

EVANS: We'll always have Praha.

McGINTY: Your job is to cross all the bridges, in any order, so long as you cross each one only once. A problem of topology.

EVANS: With you on the wing, looking down and noting my every step.

McGINTY: When were you last in Prague?

EVANS: I know it as the Thirteen Schoolgirls Problem.

McGINTY: When did you last cross the river?

EVANS: Thirteen schoolgirls step out at playtime on seven successive days, three or four abreast, and each wants new partners, to be abreast of different girls on each new day. And who doesn't?

McGINTY: On the Emperor Charles Bridge?

EVANS: Hermione, Lavinia, Abigail and Little Jo.

McGINTY: Or the Emperor Franz Bridge?

EVANS: Lisbet, Emmie, Charlotte and Pru. Dear old Pru.

McGINTY: Chalking the door of the toll-booth.

EVANS: Which side?

McGINTY: Of the river?

EVANS: Of the door. Inside or out?

McGINTY: Did you ever use the footbridge?

The lights blink once.

EVANS: Violet, Elsie and Olive. I'm struggling here.

McGINTY: The chain-link footbridge.

EVANS: Felicity. Felicity and one other.

McGINTY: We want you leaving just the one set of footprints.

EVANS: We?

McGINTY: Or none. Did you cycle across the footbridge?

EVANS: I was never in Prague.

Blackout. Lights up. EVANS *alone.*

EVANS: It was in Prague. At the height. My watch set an hour-and-a-half slow. I'd set out at midnight and walk the bridges in my soft shoes. Using my chalk. Sparingly. Two dog-ends at the bottom of the Castle steps squashed into an X. I tell a lie. It was Kaliningrad. And Kitty. That was her name. Kitty the thirteenth.

Blackout. Lights up. McGINTY *alone. Looks left.*

McGINTY: Yes.

Blackout.

Oliver Reynolds's *Hodge* was published by Areté*Books*.

Craig Raine

Kafka's Deconstructed Narratives

Kafka's diary for 6 August 1914: 'my penchant for portraying my dream-like inner life has rendered everything else inconsequential.'

A definition: deconstruction is the state of perfect contradiction, of semantic polarity.

A metaphor: deconstruction is two dogs after an act of intercourse, inextricably joined at the genitals, pulling in opposite directions, trying to go their separate ways.

A mistake: to believe deconstruction is incoherence, semantic chaos. Classic deconstruction is the demonstration of an elegant theorem, of a perfect dialectic – the coexistence of exact opposites. Beauty and the beast: p and not-p in logic, where p stands for proposition. Deconstruction is designed to show that language is unfit for purpose by demonstrating, not incoherence, but coherent incoherence.

Kafka writes deconstructed narratives.

Example: in Kafka's story, 'A Country Doctor', the narrator is an old medical practitioner who has to journey by gig to visit a patient. When he reaches the patient, however, nothing is amiss: 'I confirmed what I already knew; the young man was quite sound, something a little wrong with his circulation, saturated by coffee by his solicitous mother, but sound and best turned out of bed with one shove.' However, on a second examination, several minutes later, the doctor-narrator's mind is changed: 'this time I discovered that the young man was indeed ill. In his right side, near the hip, was an open wound as big as the palm of my hand.' So, a substantial wound, unaccountably missed, and now described in detail: 'Rose-red, in many variations of shade, dark in the grooves, lighter at the edges, softly granulated, with irregular clots of blood, open as a surface-mine to the daylight.' On yet closer examination, the wound is worm-infested: 'worms, as thick and long as my little finger.'

Sound and profoundly corrupted. Hale and in mortal danger. This is classic deconstruction, opposites that remind us of the irresistible operations of dream – the sensations of gratification and frustration, of insuperable problems and arbitrary solutions, of enigma and inventive, improvised explanation.

The key to Kafka is dream – dream in which narrative deliquescence is disguised by precision. For example, the precise topography of that wound and its population of worms.

In Beckett, the prose exhibits its morbid *je m'enfoutisme* for the purpose of bleak comedy. It revels in its torpid disarray: the prose is a species of automatic writing, hardly required to make sense since Beckett is fully persuaded of art's exhaustion.

Kafka is different. One epistemological state is succeeded by another which insists on its plausibility. And Kakfa knows that dreams are engines of interchangeability. They can be comic. They can be horrifying. The dream is various. Sometimes its untruths encompass truth.

In 'The Judgment', the narrator consults his aged parent about a friend in Russia to whom he has written. At first, his father questions the existence of this friend and accuses his son of pulling his leg. Later, the father is derisory, boasting that he has had extensive correspondence with the friend, who values the father's letters while crumpling the letters of the son, unread. Thus: 'Do you really have this friend in St Petersburg?' Two pages later: 'in his left hand he [the friend] crumples your letters unopened while in his right hand he holds up my letters to read through!'

When the son George initially enters his father's sitting room, 'his father was sitting by the window in a corner hung with various mementoes of George's dead mother, *reading a newspaper* which he held to one side before his eyes in an attempt to overcome a defect of vision.' [my italics] Three pages later: 'Do you think I read the newspapers?' the father demands, 'and he threw George a newspaper sheet which had somehow found its way into his bed. An old newspaper, with a name entirely unknown to George.'

So 'The Judgment' shares a fundamental mechanism with 'A Country Doctor'. I have deliberately selected my examples for clarity, but selection subtly violates the texture of these stories, which are kinetic. They seem stable – that first 'enormous' newspaper, strangely, convincingly held to assist a defect of vision. But on closer inspection there is constant movement, a shiftiness, oneiric shape-changing. It is like the cathedral foundations in Golding's novel *The Spire*:

> Then, as Jocelin looked, he saw a pebble drop with two clods of earth; and immediately a patch of perhaps a yard square fell out of the side below him and struck the bottom with a soft thud. The pebbles that fell with it lay shining dully in the reflected light, and settled themselves in their new bed. But as he watched them and waited for them to settle, the hair rose on the nape of his neck; for they never settled completely. He saw one stir, as if with sudden restlessness; and the he saw that they were all moving more or less, with a slow stirring, like the stirring of grubs. The earth was moving under the grubs, urging them this way and that, like porridge coming to boil in a pot; and the grubs were made to crawl by it, as dust will crawl on the head of a tapped drum.

Those grubs are like the worms in the wound – invisible, then visible.

In 'A Country Doctor', there are no horses to pull the doctor's gig. The doctor's horse has died. Then two magnificent horses are led out of the pig-sty. It takes only a moment to arrive at his destination. The return journey takes forever: 'never shall I reach home at this rate.'

In 'The Judgment', George's father 'is still a giant of a man'. Yet he is 'toothless' and stands 'feebly enough'. George carries 'his father to bed in his arms'.

In *Death in the Afternoon*, Hemingway analyses a photograph of a horse being gored by a bull. The horse's face is impassive because, Hemingway says, it believes the knees of the picador, which are calming and re-assuring. The rider is over-riding the catastrophe taking place. Readers of Kafka are in a similar position. At every juncture we are persuaded. The plainness of Kafka's prose style, the absence of metaphor, serve to lull the reader. They are the picador's knees persuading us that nothing unusual is occurring.

And there is a calculated unreadability also. We might compare its operation with blinders or blinkers on that horse. Kafka's prose is like the Bible before it was divided into chapter and verse. It is virtually without paragraphs and therefore without pause. It doesn't allow for reflection. We overlook the contradictions in Kafka because his fiction is predicated on reader amnesia. In *Testaments Betrayed*, Milan Kundera says the lyric poet has an advantage over the novelist – because all his words are remembered, whereas the novel is being forgotten almost as fast as we read it. And yet the novelist writes as if he were a lyric poet, expecting his readers to recall every word. A vain hope. Kafka takes this disadvantage and makes it an advantage. It is an important technical feat. He *wants* us to forget, to read and to welter in the calibrated, precise, insoluble confusion that is the dense Kafka experience.

Kafka used this trope of contradiction, this about-face, with fluent, practised expertise. But though Kafka's technique was so practised, so habitual, so second-nature, he was baffled by 'The Judgment'. For him, this story seems to have been exceptional and troubling. He describes the experience of reading it aloud to friends: 'towards the end my hand was moving uncontrollably and right in front of my face. I had tears in my eyes. The indubitability of the story was confirmed.' In a letter to Felice (3 June 1913), Kafka asks: 'Are you finding any meaning in "The Judgment", I mean some straightforward, coherent meaning that can be followed? I am not finding any and I am also unable to explain anything in it.' Again, I think we have to consider the nature of dream. Not simply its operations, but its after-shock. In *Wuthering Heights*, Cathy asks Nelly Dean if she ever has those dreams that colour subsequent waking existence: 'I've dreamt in my life dreams that have stayed with me ever after, and changed my ideas: they've gone through and through me, like wine through water, and altered the colour of my mind.' We all of us harbour a prejudice that dreams are more than nonsense – that they contain meaning. Kafka wants to know the meaning of this dream he has written.

Kafka was obsessed by his father. And this oneiric story is steeped in home truths – truths of usurpation, of misprision, of quenched power, of authority subdued but not inert. Essentially, it is a story in which the father rebels like an adolescent son. It is a power struggle between parent and child, conducted with politeness and the appearance of consideration. The father is happy in the darkness and airlessness of his room. That is how he prefers it. The son, however, will press improvements on his father, politely, implacably, deafly. Combustion is inevitable. Finally, the father condemns the son to death by drowning. And here Kafka gifts us an incomparable, comic detail: the narrator, above the water, swings himself over the railings, 'like the distinguished gymnast he had once been in his youth, to his parents' pride'.

'The Great Wall of China' is a parable of knowledge, of our epistemological discontinuities. The wall is built in sections of a thousand yards. There are several explanations of why this should be so – all of them provisional and many implausible. For example, the idea that greater lengths, always far from completion, would be demoralising for the work-force. Or the idea that a sense of personal responsibility was essential to the 'leaders', if not to the labour-force.

In life, we 'know' many things without knowing them first-hand. And there are many, many things we do not know. There are Donald Rumsfeld's much-mocked known unknowns and his unknown unknowns. Assertions about the Great Wall cannot, in Kafka's parable, be verified, 'at least by any single man with his own eyes and judgement, on account of the extent of the structure'. Philosophers call this contextualism. A true sceptic would be intellectually paralysed by these uncertainties. We choose not to question much of our knowledge. In other cultures, however, some of these assumptions seem improbable. In his poem 'Chosun', James Fenton itemises several cultural assumptions in ancient Korea, like the idea that the world was flat, 'Hooked on to eternity in some way by the corners'. The city is a boat, so to dig for water would sink the boat: 'Therefore to dig wells was treason.' The Great Wall of China is another culture, chosen by Kafka to alert our scepticism.

In our own culture, our scepticism is lethargic. An example near to hand. This is the author note to the Vintage edition of Kafka's *America*: 'His unhappy love affairs, his difficult relationship with his father, and his own inflexible honesty and intense sensitivity combined to weaken his health and in 1917 he discovered he was suffering from tuberculosis.' Not a flat world attached by its corners to eternity, but an equally absurd myth accepted by credulous readers. Who ever thought that honesty carried a health risk? What we have here is several thousand-yard sections of biography fused into a single factoid.

What has this, what has 'The Great Wall of China' to do with dream? This: in life we proceed, *as we do in dreams*, on trust, on unwarranted certainty. 'Hymn from a Watermelon Pavilion', a poem by Wallace Stevens, sums it up:

> Of the two dreams, night and day,
> What lover, what dreamer, would choose
> The one obscured by sleep?

All readers of Kafka owe a great debt to Milan Kundera, who has freed Kafka from solemnity. In 'Dialogue on the Art of Composition' (in *The Art of the Novel*), he places Kafka among the surrealists, his novels a 'seamless fusion of dream and reality'. In *Testaments Betrayed* (Section

8 of 'The Castrating Shadow of Saint Garta'), Kundera invokes André Breton's *Surrealist Manifesto* and its call for the 'eventual fusion of these two states, dream and reality'. The example given is the chance encounter of an umbrella with the sewing machine. Kundera says clearly that this heralded fusion had *already* occurred in Kafka's fiction. What for Kundera emerges from this fusion of dream and reality is *surprise*, or the 'density of unexpected encounters'. In *The Curtain*, Kundera advances and develops his argument thus: by fusing reality and dream, Kafka empties reality of its plausibility, its reason. Reality approaches the Absurd as we find it in Sartre's *La Nausée.*

Which isn't what I mean at all. I think Kafka is primarily interested in the literary possibilities of dream itself – and dream's alternative reality, with its permanent *sensation* of sense that co-exists with the arbitrary and the contradictory. The sensation of sense I speak of would be vulnerable were Kafka once to concede implicitly that his narratives took place in dream conditions. When we dream, we do not know we are dreaming.

Matthew Francis

Kafka's 'The Married Couple'

A businessman is addressing us. Business is bad, he tells us, so much so that he has taken to calling on his customers in person. We never learn what this business is, though he is clearly selling something physical, since he refers to his 'case of samples'. This being a short story, we are given no more information than we need; this being Kafka, we begin to suspect by the end that he is giving us a bit less than that. None of the five characters has a name: the narrator's client comes nearest to one, with just an initial, N, which sounds, to my middle-aged English ears, like the N or M of the Book of Common Prayer – standing for *Name* or *Nomen*. N, the client, is an unknown quantity, and the narrator tells us as much: his 'business relations' with this man have lapsed, for reasons he doesn't understand, and so he resolves to call at N's house in an effort to put things right.

Something else in short supply is dialogue. There are only three lines of it in the whole story. Almost all the speech is reported speech – the narrative is a summary, telling rather than showing, to use the terminology of the creative writing class, filtered through the narrator's consciousness. We get the incidents he thinks important told in his words and reflecting his interests and prejudices, monologue replacing dialogue. And his concerns, as he told us at the outset, are those of a businessman. This is a story about business versus the personal sphere, related by a man who can't help letting the one get in the way of the other. He has decided to call at N's house, rather than his workplace, and at an unbusinesslike hour. All the tensions and mysteries stem from that.

There is a crisis at N's house: his son is sick and his parents are at the bedside. N, an old man, is unwell himself: he has just come in, tired and distressed. The speaker sees all this – in fact, as we are to learn by the end, he is far from insensitive, not a Pythonesque bowler-hatted caricature with no understanding of the personal sphere at all – but what almost crowds it out of his consciousness is the presence of a business rival, 'the agent', at the sick man's bedside. This provokes him to a frenzy of salesmanship. He begins to walk up and down, making his pitch, though, we don't get to hear what he says, only his reflections on it: 'I was myself alarmed by the concessions I granted, concessions that had not even been asked for.' In this dialogueless world, we see the scene in dumbshow, a series of actions that, deprived of their natural soundtrack, come across as absurd, the agent repeatedly putting his hat on and taking it off again in a gesture as inappropriate to the domestic context as the speaker's striding, N twisting uncomfortably in his chair, the son alarmingly sitting up and shaking his fist.

Then, still in dumbshow, N dies. Only the speaker, it seems, both understands this and is able to respond to it. The son retreats under the bedclothes; the wife, putting away her husband's coat, is out of the room. It will fall to the speaker to break the news to her – death, after all, has its business aspect, too, and someone has to take charge of it.

It is as if Frau N brings her husband back to life again, by doing what no one else has done in this story, speaking a line of dialogue. 'He's fallen asleep,' she says, and, though our immediate response is to pity her misapprehension, it turns out to be true. For a moment the universe seems to flow backwards, the laws of the material world cancelled at a word – but it is just another human being briefly cutting through the hard outer covering of the speaker's personality to reveal what is actually happening. Then we are back in dumbshow mode, as N exaggeratedly reads the newspaper, clicks his tongue and lies down in his son's bed. It is only now that we realise we are reading a comedy.

The speaker, I have claimed, is not insensitive: he's just someone who has let the business side of his life get in the way of the personal side at the wrong time and in the wrong place. Now, woken by dialogue and, at the same time, by femininity (in the story's historical context, after all, business and femininity were not supposed to have much to do with each other), he makes exactly the opposite mistake. The whole of his repressed personal side comes rushing back at once, in the form of a speech to Frau N that gloriously conflates childhood, guilt, femininity, bereavement and a pre-rational belief in the miraculous. She reminds him of his mother, he tells her: 'Whatever people say, she could do wonders. Things that we destroyed she could make whole again. I lost her when I was still a child.' What is she supposed to make of this? Actually, she can't make anything of it because she is deaf, and besides she has very little idea who he is, having confused him with the agent.

If 'The Married Couple' had been written in any other way, from another point of view or in the third person, or just with more dialogue, it would have been an entirely different story. One is tempted to say, more simply, it would have been a story, because it comes close to not being one. Whatever is going on in that bedroom, in the lives of N, his wife, his son and the agent of a rival business concern, we never really understand; we watch it as if on a television with the sound turned off because the person who tells us about it is so busy talking that he does not hear anything anyone else says. But when a word does get through, the effect on the speaker's perceptions is so devastating that, for a moment, we slip into a different genre altogether: suddenly it's a snippet of delusory magic realism (by the author of *Metamorphosis*) about a man's resurrection. In his speech to Frau N, he desperately tries to put the ingredients of another story together: the long-neglected tale of his own childhood, of whatever was destroyed that his mother put back together again, and of how he lost her. But it is too late now to tell it, and there is no sympathetic female ear to listen. He has condemned himself to a narrative outside the personal sphere, without the logic of plot and closure. Modernist literature, perhaps most obviously in the work of Beckett, was soon to make familiar the rueful tragicomic note of that anti-ending: 'Oh, how many business calls come to nothing, and yet one must keep going.'

Matthew Francis's latest book of poems, *Muscovy*, was published by Faber in 2013.

Areté
FICTION

Oliver Rowse

Kafka: Raptures of Anxiety

The false start, the promising fragment, the contentedly tiny whole: three categories into which we might divide the creative efforts of Kafka's 'diaries'. 'Notebooks' would be more matter-of-fact: the pulse of the journal is irregular at best. In certain moments the word 'ledger' comes to mind, for Kafka likes to account his heaviest doubts, to declare every scruple and conviction. Steadiest of all are the voices of the clinician – precise, impassive – verblessly noting the day's headaches, and the artist, hysterically sober about his work and prospects.

One element is strikingly scarce: material, in crude form, fictional antematter. Where, carefully anthologised, is the birdsong of bureaucracy, so distinctive in Kafka's dreamworlds? Where is the train-carriage conversation, discreetly, hurriedly, shakily transcribed? Where are all the unconscious particles of everyday address, those touches of blandishment and self-importance that bring humour, and paradoxically menace, to Kafka's dialogue? And where are the views from bedroom windows and all that dwindling light, that mist? Where, *mein Gott*, is the love of *nature*, pure and simple, in all its forms, the sketches of bugs, notes on moles, dogs, horses etc?

To open Kafka's diaries is to enter, not a larder, well stocked with fictional ingredients, but a deserted kitchen, terminus of a thousand abandoned soufflés. Kafka had a weakness for beginnings, it seems, and hardly ever the strength for an ending:

> Tired of working in other people's stores, I had opened up a little stationery store of my own. Since my means were limited and I had to pay cash for almost everything –

Another foundling:

> Two friends went for a morning ride.

Then, miraculously, a perfect bauble:

> 'Don't you want to join us?' I was recently asked by an acquaintance when he ran across me alone after midnight in a coffee-house that was almost deserted. 'No, I don't,' I said.

Perhaps all this concoction explains the relative absence of 'raw material'; the stories are the start rather than the result of any gathering. In their beginning is their invention. Only then do they begin to dredge themselves from Kafka's dreamlife, in a process central to Kafkan mythology: the inspiration bender, the museathon.

Updike said of his own stories:

> Most came right the first time – rode on their own melting, as Frost said of his poems. If there is no melting, if the story keeps sticking, better stop and look around. In the execution there has to be a 'happiness' that can't be willed or foreordained. It has to sing, click, something. I try instantly to set in motion a certain forward tilt of suspense or curiosity, and at the end of the story or novel to rectify the tilt, to complete the motion.

Kafka, with the special vehemence of self-loathing, would surely agree. He knows adventure and misadventure. The account of the single sitting which produced 'The Judgment' resounds with the boisterousness and superbity of elation, the diary entry itself dashed off in giddy staccato ('How it turned blue outside the window. A wagon rolled by. Two men walked across the bridge.'), giving its melodramatic turn. Yet in the triumphant resolve that follows we see hubris: 'Only *in this way*,' writes Kafka, with emphasis, 'can writing be done, only with such coherence, with such a complete opening out of the body and the soul.' All too true, it transpires, in Kafka's case, and more's the pity: Kafka knows a story's thrillingly unpredictable advance, its intricately surreal fandango, but he knows best of all its sticky, unhappy dead-end.

Writing quickly and continuously in happy spells, disenchanted just as suddenly – the story before him transforming, at self-conscious break of day, from beauty into beast – is it any wonder that Kafka's image is crossed with mysticism? Add a little isolation and privation and ill health and neurosis and self-obsession and things are looking anchoritic. But just as it is now well-known that Kafka was not fit for the category of sainthood, his best stories are not the pure expression of beatitude, or indeed luck: both categories belittle the importance of instinct, a less divine but no less mysterious force than inspiration.

When K first meets his assistants in *The Castle*, they salute him. Kafka says of K:

> Remembering his army days, those happy times, he gave a laugh.

The biographical detail is tiny, gratuitous, and yet we glimpse a history. Its effect is to distract, momentarily, from the present focus of the fiction, giving, as it does, onto K's past. And to reconnect, again momentarily, the increasingly singular fantasy in which K is ensnared with the more banal reality of army service; to illuminate, like a flashbulb, his situation's present perversity. The concision of the aperture is also important; the detail works, and thrills, like a peepshow. Kafka's prose is full of such disruptive, corrective, even rebellious touches – pertly responsive, unmistakably spontaneous, each an unexpected leap of instinct. To be diverted or side-stepped by instinct is one of the prose's major exhilarations.

Witness also how the stories germinate. And more often than not it is from *small* beginnings. The worried voice, speaking. The tableau, as here:

> The Negroes came out of the thicket. They leaped into a dance which they performed around a wooden stake encircled by a silver chain. The priest sat to one side, a little rod raised above the gang. The sky was overcast and silent; no rain fell.

Which has all the punctiliousness of stage direction, and yet contains something greater than geometry. Some charge, some set of tensions is coded here that fix our curiosity. Kafka's diaries are foremost a home for these ravelled potentialities, their unwinding as mysterious to Kafka, we sense, as it remains to us. One is reminded of Pinter, another disciple of instinct, and his very Kafkaesque sense of a beginning:

> I went into a room and saw two people sitting down, and a few weeks later I wrote *The Room*. I went into another room and saw two people sitting down, and a few years later I wrote *The Birthday Party*. I looked through a door into a third room, and saw two people standing up and I wrote *The Caretaker*.

Pinter is being droll, but it is at this level – the level of the tableau, the exchange, the fragment – that his imagination, like Kafka's, is fecund. And on such simple, striking, solid kernels that his imagination likes to suck. They contain a forward tilt, to use Updike's phrase, that must be expressed and followed. Whether the result will be a dramatic or shapely is impossible to predict. Kafka is less homely in his determinism than Updike, and thinks in terms of the eugenicist: 'the story, if it has any justification to exist, bears its complete organisation within itself even before it has been fully formed.' The Kafka story starts life, or so his diaries declare, as a striking but mysterious organism that wants observation. Kundera notes that many of the stories are reducible to jokes, but this is not to say they necessarily begin in the test tube of conceit. The punch line to 'A Hunger-Artist' – that the Hunger-Artist's feats of starvation were really a consequence of pickiness, not denial – would make an elegant hypothesis. But did Kafka pursue hypotheses? The evidence suggests that Kafka would rather attend his stories than plan them; would rather follow them than urge them on. In this we sense again the primacy of instinct, instinct before design.

Dispensing quickly, if at all, with introductions, his stories simply set off, enigmatic and assured – their assurance augmented, in turn, by enigma. Indeed, however mazily a story continues, its telling is almost always direct, essential; even, in the fervour of its momentary focus, forgetful. It is unusual for Kafka's stories to look back, to recap, even to pause. To make sense of themselves, in other words. They are more often to be found facing the future, in raptures of anxiety, speculation, or else engrossed in the nosebag of the present, in report. Their charisma is an introvert charisma; their self-possession self-absorbed.

Still, what makes a Kafka story stick? Or why does he stub one out, just lit or half-smoked, in distaste? These questions address instinctive wrong-turns and abortions, but also delicacies of Kafka's style. Kafka made something of a study of these – not so much weaknesses as susceptibilities. This diary entry of 9 February 1915 is typical:

> Just now read the beginning. It is ugly and gives me a headache. In spite of all its truth it is wicked, pedantic, mechanical, a fish barely breathing on a sandbank. I write my *Bouvard et Pécuchet* prematurely. If the two elements – most pronounced in 'The Stoker' and 'In the Penal Colony' – do not combine, I am finished. But is there any prospect of their combining?

Kafka worries about this measure – truth – in a variety of terms. 'But,' he says, self-persuasively, of another story, 'it has more reality than anything I have written his past year.' Truth, *reality* – next to mechanism, pedantry, wickedness – these things stand for something more vivid than verisimilitude, which, after all, would include mechanism and pedantry and wickedness as they are part of life. Something not to be got at through sheer volume of detail, through the sort of notation to which Kafka's style is prone. (Impedimenta, really, which belong to Kafka's mechanical, pedantic, wicked side.) Nor, by the way, should this quantity – truth, reality – be understood as the source of Kafka's strength, but in combination with his mechanical, pedantic, wicked tendencies, which give Kafka's dreamworlds their perverted rigour and deviant logic. Truth, in Kafka's sense, is achieved more laconically; it has a gleam that notation dulls. As when the hunger-artist, on the point of death, raises his head and speaks into the overseer's ear, 'with his lips puckered as if in a kiss'. Or the potatoes in the supper scene of 'The Metamorphosis', which 'steamed mightily'. These effects are of the same caste as the gratuitous biographical touch from *The Castle*. They enlarge and mollify Kafka's worlds, which would otherwise, left to their own mechanical, pedantic and wicked devices, become narrow and vicious. 'The horror in the merely schematic,' as a note in the *Diaries* puts it. This truthful–mechanical tension is essential to the artistic vigour of Kafka's work; when this combination does not come off, the result is worse, or, we presume, unfinished.

Another related susceptibility is incoherence. Kafka's plots, even at their most complete, are errant. Some work like mirages. At their most degraded they tantalise predictably, monotonously, like horizons. K arrives in the village intending to visit the Castle. He is frustrated. Frustrated, he sets about removing the petty obstacle to his first intention. And so on. Purpose, frustration, derivative purpose – a dialectic we observe most distinctly at the beginning of the novel. But it is not the novel's only mode. K's sense of purpose does not ramify in such an inbred way: he is just as likely to be interrupted, distracted, enlisted; he is just as likely to forget what it was he wanted in the first place. Even such is life. Telos is never so fixed or incorruptible as it is in drama, a principle that Kafka's fiction exaggerates at infernal length. In the variety and fluidity of his resolutions, K is effectively irresolute. But at its least sequential, at its most entropic, this kind of plot endangers, or perhaps exhausts the reader's curiosity, his suspense glands. This consideration worried Kafka. 'How do I intend to solder fragments together into a story that will sweep one along?' he wrote while engaged in the Amalia section of *The Castle*.

His question happens upon another tension in Kafka's fiction: between the unity and the logic of dramatic action on the one hand, artful irresolution, with its fragments and logical lacunae, on the other. Between soldering scenes and preserving the separate pregnancy of each enigmatic tableau, the sprung mislogic of their succession. Between closing a story off and keeping it suggestible. We might refer this tension to the previous tension: to think in terms of orderly, mechanical plot and erratic, truthful fragmentation.

* * *

A great variety must be admitted in the body of Kafka's fiction, a great many factions under the banner of Kafkaesque. A great unevenness in quality too. Kafka, as we know, was satisfied with little he wrote, and one is tempted to take him seriously. Under pressure from Brod to deliver *Meditation* to Rowohlt, the eventual publisher, he confessed he could not 'clear up the little pieces that still remain'. Why? Because they had not yielded their design? Is the difference between those stories with which Kafka was dissatisfied and not dissatisfied a question of their not being finished, or botched?

In any case what a gulf there is in intricacy, in ambition, and in result, between the loose-ended, epiphanic prose poems of *Meditation* – an effort like 'The Plight of the Bachelor', say – or even the later, more self-contained stories of *A Country Doctor*, and a story like 'The Metamorphosis'. Kafka's great stories resemble these smaller, lesser attempts, whether finished, unfinished, pretending to be finished, only in so far as we recognise certain painterly habits: the deliberation over individual objects and foregrounds, faces, and the lax simplicity of his backgrounds, his job descriptions – a contrast that produces a lurid signature.

And yet the great stories are of a different artistic order altogether, with ironies as thoroughly exfoliated as any in Henry James, changes as wrung as those in a Woody Allen. They have a complexity and coherence unmatched in the shorter prose – equally unmatched in a novel of fragments like *The Castle*. One such is 'The Metamorphosis', another is 'In the Penal Colony'.

* * *

'In the Penal Colony' was first completed during a holiday that Kafka took from the beginning of October, 1914. He returned to its ending in 1917; the *Diaries* preserve alternative endings composed at the beginning of August in that year. Quite how the story looked in 1914 is obscure. What is important is that Kafka thought it finished, as he recorded in an uncharacteristic summary of the year's work on New Year's Eve, 1914:

> Finished only: 'In the Penal Colony' and a chapter of *Der Verschollene* [*America*], both during the two-week holiday.

The story satisfies Kafka's truthful–mechanical formula in quite a concrete sense. At its centre is a machine, whose complex operation and history are explained during the first half of the narrative. The machine gives physical form to the mechanical, the pedantic, the wicked. Around it turns reality, truth: a man is due to be executed by the machine, a simple action that gives the story its course. Attending his punishment are a traveller, who has come to the penal colony purely to observe its justice system, a soldier, whose job it is to guard the condemned man, and the officer, who facilitates and explains the working of the machine – an *apparatchik*, in the literal sense of that word. It is with these four – in their response to the machine – that the drama of the story rests: a struggle not so much between man and machine as between the human and the mechanical.

On rereading, we find in the story's first paragraph, which sets the scene of the execution, a sketch of the story's design and a suggestion of its dominant notes. It is a sort of *argumentum*, as one might find at the beginning of an antique poem:

> The traveller seemed to have taken up the commandant's invitation merely out of politeness, when he asked if he would like to be present at the execution of a soldier, who

> had been condemned for insubordination and insulting an officer. Interest in the execution seemed not to be that great in the penal colony either.

Knowing Kafka's beginnings, and finding the story's donné so conspicuously and so entirely here, it is not difficult to imagine the paragraph as the fragment whose gestation produced the whole, as if all that followed were an effort to decode the above. The execution is of a 'soldier', the first of many ironies: an instrument, at least nominally, of the penal system, not a victim. Indeed, we do not meet an indentured or even non-official inhabitant until the very end of the story. The penal system, Kafka suggests at the outset, eats its own, eats itself.

The traveller, our surrogate in the penal colony, is, perhaps as we are at the beginning, 'indifferent'. He is there 'out of politeness' – an instinct as important in the story's scheme as morality, whose inflammations it sedates. The officer then begins his description of the machine, 'the brainchild of our previous commandant', and describes its parts: the bed, the engraver and the harrow. The traveller finds himself warming to the officer's enthusiasm as he relates in French – 'a language neither the soldier nor the condemned man could possibly have understood' – how the condemned man lies face-down on the cotton-wool-covered bed, takes a felt stump in his mouth (to stifle screams and prevent him biting off his own tongue), before the bed is set in motion and the harrow begins to carry out the sentence.

The sentence, the officer explains, is to be inscribed by many needles onto the body the condemned man – in this case, 'Respect your commanding officer!' Sadomasochism to a Hell's Angel, but essentially one long fatal tattoo. Turning to the condemned man and deciding that 'the movements of his blubbery pressed lips showed that quite evidently he had not managed to glean anything', the traveller asks whether he knows his sentence. He doesn't, the officer explains, 'It will be put to him physically' – a comeback all the more comic and – again the paradox – all the more frightening for its cordial, even forbearing matter-of-factness. Which invites some probing of the colony's legal system, a system stupendously inverted: there is no opportunity for defence in the penal colony's legal procedure, for instance, because defence would entail confusion (contradiction); the principle on which the system depends – 'guilt is always beyond doubt' – is central to its expedition.

At this point the traveller, whose moral sensibility, retarded by complaisance, works a crucial one phase behind the reader's, registers his own 'unsatisfaction'; but remembers, almost in the same semi-thought, that he is only a visitor, an observer, in these parts. The officer continues his description of the sentence, which he embellishes reverentially. Its duration is twelve hours. (To put this in context, Christ managed nine on the cross.) Around the sixth the condemned man 'understands'. At the twelfth hour the process proves fatal.

The officer proudly produces 'sketches', drawn by the old commandant, which the harrow follows in its inscription. The traveller, though he 'would have liked to say something complimentary', pronounces them illegible; the officer concedes they take time to read. 'Of course, the writing mustn't be too straightforward; it's not supposed to be fatal straight away ... And many ornaments surround the script proper; the actual text is traced round the body like a narrow belt; the rest of the body is set aside for decoration.'

So far, so satirical: a system in which sentence and punishment, understanding and contrition, are fatally conflated; a system, in short, where everything legal has become penal; a system whose operation is mechanically transparent and yet beyond comprehension to all save its officiators, and especially obscure to those it affects; a system whose language accommodates and indeed enshrines decoration, superfluity, while what it needs to communicate remains illegible. The significance of the title begins to dawn on us: the penal colony is not simply a place for the punished, but a place that makes punishment a religion, an art.

All of which has satire's strut, and little of the insidiousness common to subtler irony. One is reminded of Dickens – a writer Kafka claimed to imitate ('"The Stoker" a sheer imitation of Dickens ... It was my intention, as I now see, to write a Dickens novel') – and his 'Containing the Whole Science of Government', a set piece in *Little Dorrit*. There he depicts the Circumlocution Office, an institution dedicated to non-government – 'How not to do it' is their mantra, and the chapter's refrain. Dickens, like Kafka, inverts the purpose of the institution and simply amplifies its manner, until it is drenched in its own observances and obliquities. The conceit here is not hiding: as with Kafka's machine, its intellectual engineering is deliberately exposed. And it *is* clever. But where the Circumlocution Office remains a riff, revived periodically – an opportunity for Dickens to indulge his rhetorical genius, his taste for schemes, those patterns of prose – the machine becomes integral to the drama of 'In the Penal Colony'. Integral because of its ambivalence – it is both barbaric and sophisticated – and because its justice remains in question.

The story's second movement begins when the condemned man is stripped and strapped. Theory gives way to practice, and vivid pedantry cedes to applied ethics. We look, naturally, to the traveller; our anxiety to know whether he will intervene is compelling. Kafka takes care to state his position, and its revisions, at every turn. The prospect of intervening – of condemning the execution – an act his status prohibits, is 'enticing':

> The injustice and the inhumanity of the execution were incontestable. No one could claim any self-interest on the part of the traveller, because the condemned man was a stranger to him, not a compatriot, and by no means a sympathetic fellow either.

Is his judgment, the traveller wonders, obscurely being sought by the new regime, which has received him with such 'politeness'.

Any verdict is suddenly prorogued when the condemned man is sick over the machine. Talking as he cleans the machine, the officer is overtaken with nostalgia for the ancien regime, and begins his lament by admitting that he is the only remaining supporter of the old commandant's system. The traveller will feel easier at the prospect of intervening, we imagine. But in a brilliant turn, Kafka has the officer solicit the traveller. He asks him, in confidence, to use his influence as a disinterested party, and to support the old system by not condemning it – by being evasive. The traveller replies:

> 'But how could I ... it's completely impossible. I am as little able to help as to harm you.'

Even as he refuses the officer, his politeness will not allow him to condemn; he is, ironically, evading the officer's question in exactly the manner the officer hopes he will evade the new commandant's. Undeterred, the officer sets off once more into fantasy, as vividly as he went about describing of the old system's glory days. He imagines the scene at court (a setting antithetical to the now empty valley that contains the machine) as the traveller abjures. Making a final plea, he breaks off.

At which point Kafka calls the traveller and we see, at last, his hand:

> The answer he had to give was not at any time in doubt for the traveller; he had experienced too much in the course of a lifetime for him to start vacillating now; he was basically

> an honest man, and he knew no fear.

Even so, when he finally condemns the execution he is politeness itself, assuring the officer that he will keep his confidence. The officer's final act is to free the condemned man, before committing himself to the machine. His sentence: 'Be just!' The traveller looks on, benumbed, once again, by propriety – 'he had no right to interfere with anything the officer was minded to do' – apparently satisfied by the logic of this reversal. He is only appalled when the collapse of the machine spoils 'torture of the kind the officer wanted to achieve'. The traveller's transposition, from observer, through witness, through interrogator, through judge, to officer, is complete.

The action breaks off. We come to the coda, and with it a change of scene, and so perspective, as radical as that in 'Metamorphosis'. It is essentially the same effect: a release. Release from their flat, in the case of the Samsas, who go for a walk; from the scene of execution, in the case of the three remaining characters of 'In the Penal Colony'. They come to a tea-house, *the* tea-house referred to earlier; a place, according to the officer, where supporters of the old regime are to be found. Though obviously run-down, to the traveller 'it still evoked a sense of history in the traveller, and he sensed the might of earlier times'. He is shown the grave of the old commandant, who was buried here when his burial in a cemetery was refused. We meet our first non-officials, 'probably port workers, strongly built men with short, gleaming black beards'. They smile at the inscription on the old commandant's gravestone, expecting that the traveller too will find it ridiculous. It ends:

> It is prophesied that after a certain number of years, the commandant will rise again, and from these premises here, lead his followers on to the reconquest of the colony. Believe and be patient!

The traveller, though, is once again inscrutable. He simply, politely, 'feigns unawareness'. He leaves and walks down to the port to book his place on a steamer. The soldier and condemned man, detained by acquaintances, catch up with him just as his boat is leaving shore. The story's final lines offer an image of aversion, of renunciation – of uninnocent abstention – that represents the traveller's ultimate condemnation:

> It was just possible for them both still to have leaped into

> the boat, but the traveller picked up a heavy knotted rope, with which he threatened them and so dissuaded them from jumping.

* * *

'Curiously enough, one cannot *read* a book: one can only reread it,' Nabokov proposes, not altogether archly, in his essay 'Good Readers and Good Writers'. But is it possible to reread a book without having *read* it? Or, to be plain, in this case: is it possible to appreciate 'In the Penal Colony' without an account of first impressions? As great art must, it works first time round. Works in a way it will never quite work again, of course, the aura of suspense never so immanent as it was on our first visit. We are unsure which force – morality or politeness – will prevail with the traveller. The righteousness of our own convictions is a luxury; but Kafka traces the duress that the social instinct places on those convictions so plausibly. It would be easy to forget too our fears for the traveller's life, which Kafka torques by upping the officer's psychotics ('the traveller noticed to his alarm that the officer had clenched his fists'), as we sense a verdict approaching. And, indeed, the accompanying horror-movie reflex: disbelief that this chump is hanging around.

The story is also coherent. Not because, as some have proposed, it is an allegory, though it partakes of the allegorical. The old commandant and the new commandant are not the respective Gods of Old and New Testament; nor do their penal systems represent predetermined and self-determined theologies; nor is their contest a contest between faith and reason; nor is the officer quite a Christ, dying for that same faith. The story is coherent on its own terms, in its own symmetries and oppositions. Just as we see the traveller's moral position inverted, so too the officer's, only in reverse, from executioner, to judge, to witness, to defendant, to victim. And just as the traveller arrives in tranquillity and leaves guilty, so the officer's self-sentence is a kind of (mangled) absolution. The condemned man, coolly uncomprehending and then submissive in respect to his own execution, is morbidly, delightedly transfixed by the officer's; he even begs – something he did not think to do in his own case – to be allowed to stay and watch. The soldier, the condemned man's keeper, is soon his friend. But the various ironic reversals do not return us to a karmic zero, which is the story's final irony: the officer's death is 'crude murder', the soldier and the condemned man are seen to 'squabble'; without the barbaric system, barbarism appears; without violence, there is no politeness.

Coherent too in its particulars: where there were once railings around the pit in the valley, there are now railings in the new commandant's court; a pair of handkerchiefs, a present from the 'ladies' (voluptuary or pitying, their influence in the story is ambiguous), are returned to the condemned man from inside the officer's tunic, where they began the story; the restraining straps which break when the condemned man is about to be executed are tied, ironically unnecessarily, when it comes to that of the officer.

The story's pedantry fascinates, and its enlivening touches bring to mind Orwell's puddle in 'A Hanging'. As when the condemned man's chains are exchanged for straps, and Kafka takes care to note 'initially, it struck the condemned man as an improvement'. Or later, having recovered his clothes, 'dreadfully soiled' and 'sliced apart up the back' from the pit, and he is having a laugh with the soldier:

> Perhaps the condemned man felt under some obligation to entertain the other, he twirled round in front of him in the cut clothing.

These moments have the counter-intuitive, the bogus feel of truth.

The officer's voice, a well-controlled routine, strikes the same truthful–mechanical balance. The enthusiastic hangman is something of a type (*Kind Hearts and Coronets, The Mikado*), and Kafka enjoys himself in fanatical impersonation, with its mania for propriety and trivia. But he is equal to the self-importance that such mania brings:

> 'It's like this. I have been appointed judge in the penal colony. In spite of my youth. Because I assisted the former commandant in all punishment-related issues, and also I have the best understanding of the machine.'

The amusing, animate touch here, surely sparked in the heat of composition? 'In spite of my youth.' Still more surprising, but suddener and more surreal, is an effect produced after the officer has made his final plea to the traveller: 'That's my plan; will you help me put it into effect? But of course you will, you must.' We hear in this the same twitter as before, perhaps more agitated now. The officer, though, is breathing heavily. 'He had yelled the last sentences at such a pitch that the soldier and the condemned man had also been alerted.' The volume corrected, we turn to replay the scene quickly in our imagination; instinct, that speedy earth-girdler, skips past us.

Kundera has made several brilliant cases for Kafka and the Kafkan (Kundera on *The Castle* is as good as *The Castle* ever gets) – memorably for Kafka's sense of the comic, his journeys into 'the dark depths of a joke'. In time a joke becomes horrible, a process of extension that Kafka's nightmares seem to understand. This holds at a remove, but does not come close to explaining the prose, many of whose comic effects are local, and whose effects, in general, are densely various. Prose in which the comic and the pathetic jostle. Bergson begins his essay *Laughter* by arguing that all comedy is fundamentally human: we do not laugh at landscape, however beautiful. Yet the laughable always involves the mechanical – the non-human – as it *encrusts* itself on the human, in Bergson's phrase. When we sense automatism in human behaviour, we laugh.

These ideas sit easier with Kafka's own truthful–mechanical diagnosis – his 'mechanical, pedantic, wicked' sensibility – and his local, prosier sense of the comic. Bergson would find comedy in a pedant like the officer. He would see the comic automatism in the traveller's politeness too. The greatness of 'In the Penal Colony', though – a greatness that explains the thrilling propinquity of tragedy and comedy in Kafka's best work – depends on its pregnable sense of the mechanical, the glimpses of self-awareness in the mist of automatism, as a character confronts, for a moment, their own rigidity. The traveller, of course, struggles with his own politeness. Does the officer feel shame? There is a moment. It follows his lament for the old days. We hear Kafka, a master of prose dynamics, hush and slow his story, clearing an acoustical sweet spot to bring what follows into full lucidity:

> The traveller wanted to turn his face from the officer, and looked aimlessly round. The officer supposed he was looking at the desert valley; he therefore seized his hands, moved round to catch his eye, and asked him: 'Do you feel it then, the disgrace?'

At the very centre of this great, crystalline story is a question, wailing, rending.

Oliver Rowse worked in publishing but is now about to start graduate work at Oxford.

Nicholas Murray

Anorexic Investigations

Towards the end of 1922, with less than 18 months left to live, Kafka wrote his story 'Investigations of a Dog'/*Forschingen eines Hundes.* Kafka's reputation – that inescapable 'Kafkaesque' – is built on novels like *The Trial* and *The Castle* but his genius is equally at home in the genre of shorter fiction. In stories like 'The Metamorphosis' or 'The Transformation', free of the occasional *longueurs* that one finds in, for instance, *The Castle,* Kafka's imaginative world exhibits a power that matches the great novels.

'Investigations of a Dog' is characteristic example of Kafka's shorter fiction but it also poses the sort of question we generally like to duck: what is it about? What does it *mean?* Were I called upon by an online encyclopaedia to provide a bluffer's summary I should flounder. Yet it is compelling, written with a quiet intensity of concentration that does not let us go, its extraordinarily long paragraphs wrapping themselves around us. Re-reading it I smiled at that point when the canine narrator declares: 'I cursed the learned art of commentary'! *Ich verfluchte die kommentatorische Wissenschaft.* Kafka has attracted learned commentators of every stripe. There cannot have been a literary critical or philosophical fashion of the last 90 years that has not had its hour with Kafka but he is still there, resisting our busy attempts to force him into one or other hermeneutic mould. That quality of resistance is part of the reason that we go on reading him.

In particular, Kafka resists attempts to decode, to identify allegorical purposes, to define the figure in the carpet. Kafka was a realist. His great story, 'The Judgment', whose writing he considered a moment of breakthrough, one in which he achieved full realisation of himself as writer (discovering 'How everything can be said. *Wie alles gesagt werden kann*') for all its provocations to the learned commentators, its symbolic freight, its elements of strangeness, was rooted in a particular time and place and in its author's actual life, overshadowed as that was by his difficult relationship with his father. When the writing was done Kafka made a 'trembling entrance' into his sister Ottla's room and read it to her. The house in the story, she declared, 'is like ours'. Kafka responded flippantly: 'In that case then Father would have to be living in the toilet.' A few months later, however, he told Felice Bauer that he himself could find no meaning in it: 'I can't find any, nor can I explain anything in it.'

Can we do any better with 'Investigations of a Dog'? Can we 'find meaning' or 'explain' it? It centres on the narrative of an 'old dog' who has retained a childlike freshness of perception, whose habit of questioning started with an incident from his childhood when he came upon a group of seven dogs near a wood who were generating a strange music. This early incident is the most dramatic moment in a largely static narrative and it became for the narrator the start of a precocious tendency to ask ceaseless questions. That inquisitiveness was not necessarily welcome to the pack who practised a kind of repressive tolerance, greeting his investigations with silence. The investigator wonders if he is seen as 'a rather cold, reserved, timid, calculating dog' and is aware of a 'fracture' in the tribal bonds that tie him to the dog pack.

As befits a dog, the chief investigation is into the science of nourishment, of where food comes from and how it is generated and delivered, and eventually this leads to what is 'perhaps the greatest achievement of my life'. This is his experiment 'to abstain entirely from eating for as long as I could' so as to perceive with total objectivity and detachment just how food presents itself to the world of the dog. He hoped that the experiment – and this clearly illustrates the bizarre imaginative world we have entered – would show how 'the nourishment from above would descend of itself and without bothering to reach the ground would tap on my teeth to be let in'. The trope of denial and self-mortification as a prelude to more truthful perception, anorexic refusal as a way to discover scientific truths, permeates this story as it permeated Kakfa's own life. He was a prodigy in the art of giving himself a bad time.

The dog's starvation-induced findings seem to promise him the possibility of a reward: 'Whereas until now I had deep down felt rejected and had stormed my people's defences like a madman, now I should be received with great honour, the warmth of the dogs' massed bodies which I had longed for would flow around me; to high acclaim I should be carried swaying on my people's shoulders.' He sees the art of hungering [*das*

Hungern] as 'the ultimate, the most powerful method in my researches. The true path goes by the way of hungering...' As it turns out there is to be no triumphant communal acceptance of the lonely truth-seeker's endeavours and the final outcome of the imposed starvation is, once again, an outbreak of music: 'everywhere I heard noise; the world that in my life so far had been asleep seemed to have been wakened by my hungering.' Moreover, this music is not the means of some primal restitution of harmony with the pack: 'the worst thing was that it seemed to be there only for me, this awe-inspiring voice, which made the forest fall silent, only for me.' It is another parable of lonely truth-seeking and alienation.

The temptation to see parallels between the dog's obsessive investigations into the nature of his universe and Kafka's similarly dogged nocturnal interrogations of life and writing that are recorded in his extraordinarily compelling diaries is hard to resist. In the end it may be the only way to make sense of this strange narrative. The reader's mind, schooled by the expectations of animal fable, naturally searches for identification of the non-human with the human. Even in the absence of intended allegory and meaningful symbol the fictional invention of a canine speaker inescapably foregrounds itself; it insists on its own artifice. Perhaps in the end we should conclude, with the investigator, that 'in the course of this, something is revealed that may not be the truth – no one will ever get that far – but at least something of the deep-rooted entanglements of the lie'.

What then does this tell us about the art of Kafka's short fiction? For the first time, re-reading this story, I felt a kind of incipient resentment at the sparse fictional gratifications that it offers. I found myself calling it 'conceptual fiction'. There is little sensuous description or evocation in this story, little colour or landscape beyond the perfunctory ('a bright day, just a bit misty'). It fails to present any deep characterisation, social complexity, or human engagement, notwithstanding its non-human premise. The dogs have vestigial communications with each other and, compelling as it is in its curious articulate energy, it is ultimately *monochrome.* Too many of the copious resources of fiction have been jettisoned.

In the end it is a piece of fiction that fascinates me but I cannot love it.

Nicholas Murray's book on Kafka was published by Little, Brown in 2004.

Our Bold

Eagleton Recycling: Moss'd Cottage Cheese

Terry Eagleton's *How to Read a Poem* (2007): 'A rather eccentric example of the incarnational fallacy can be found in F R Leavis's comments on the phrase "moss'd cottage trees" in Keats's "Ode to Autumn": "The action of the packed consonants in 'moss'd cottage trees' is plain enough: there stand the trees, gnarled and sturdy in trunk and bough, their leafy entanglements thickly loaded. It is not fanciful. I think, to find that (the sense being what it is) the pronouncing of 'cottage trees' suggests, too, the crisp bite and flow of juice as the teeth close in the ripe apple." **If this is not fanciful, it is hard to know what is.'**

Christopher Ricks's *Milton's Grand Style* (1963), quoting Leavis: '"The action of the packed consonants in 'moss'd cottage trees' is plain enough: there stand the trees, gnarled and sturdy in trunk and bough, their leafy entanglements thickly loaded. It is not fanciful. I think, to find that (the sense being what it is) the pronouncing of 'cottage trees' suggests, too, the crisp bite and flow of juice as the teeth close in the ripe apple." **But if this is not fanciful, then what is?'**

Spenglerian, wouldn't you say?

Or just postmodern theory, which, according to Eagleton, 'embraces a world in which everything is a recycled, translated, parodied or derivative version of something else'?

Eagleton making an example of himself?

Ruari Owen

Kafkaccino

On 17 March 2014, at the Linbury Studios, Covent Garden, Francisco Coll's short opera *Café Kafka* received its premiere. The libretto was by Meredith Oakes who also wrote the libretto for Thomas Adès's full-length opera based on Shakespeare's *The Tempest.* Francisco Coll has been a private pupil of Adès.

In her programme note, the librettist Meredith Oakes said she 'wound up taking sections from over a dozen' of Kafka's different stories. She didn't say which. Section 1 is taken from 'The Departure'. In Section 2, the source is 'Excursion into the mountains'. Section 3 comes from 'Description of a Struggle'. Section 4 is from 'Gracchus', as is Section 12. Sections 5 and 6 are taken from 'Rejection'. Section 7 from 'Description of a Struggle', a longish story of Kafka's which is the main source for Coll and Oakes's opera. Section 14 is based on 'Wedding Preparations in the Country'.

A cento of sorts, then. Unpromising on the page, it could be a recipe for incoherence – except that the theme of Coll's opera is fundamental incoherence. It ends with a man unable to find his way to the railway station who asks directions of a policeman. The policeman responds by telling him to give it up.

What makes these fragments cohere? It is partly the set – a glitzy cocktail bar where there are two tie-less men in suits and bare feet. Two women flirt with the men and swap partners and pick-ups. There is a lot of jaundiced chat-up. The incoherence is accounted for by the copious amounts that are drunk. We don't expect much in the way of cogent discussion. The sung dialogue has something of the headlong riffs we associate with Pinter's dramatic Tourette's. We hear about Gracchus, the hunter who has fallen from a precipice in pursuit of a chamois. The dead Gracchus has been placed in a death ship whose voyage to the other world is endlessly deferred and never concluded.

Just as the shenanigans between the couples reach an approximate conclusion, Gracchus himself crawls half-naked over the counter of the cocktail bar. Theatrically, this abrupt collision between a recognisable world (the cocktail bar) and myth (the voyaging Gracchus) is a brilliantly effective surprise, a tour de force, particularly when it morphs into the unhelpful policeman 'like someone who wants to be alone with his own laughter'.

And these Kafka fragments share a tone. The texts are all versions of nympholeptic narrative whose meaning perpetually eludes us just as we feel we are about to grasp it. Meredith Oakes understands Kafka well: 'The vertigo and intoxication people feel not just from trying and failing to understand the world, but also from trying to deal with the actual details of their own and other people's behaviour.' It is the summary of a Kafka adept. It is the shared tone that holds the fragmentary libretto together, a tone of notation and accountancy as reality suddenly turns sideways into invisibility.

The singers – Suzanne Shakespeare, Daniel Norman, Anna Dennis, William Purefoy and the rufus-haired Andri Björn Róbertsson – performed with conviction and vigour. The music was effective but oddly invisible because the stage events were so absorbing that the normal sound world of opera was reversed. Usually, the voices struggle to be heard above the orchestra. Here, the voices were piercingly dominant and the band made its contribution, but elusively, leaving hardly a trace behind it. As if it too were a kind of orchestral nympholepsy. I thought of Joyce's 'Calypso', where traditional notions of background and foreground are reversed, where the plot is the letter from Blazes Boylan that Molly Bloom hides under her pillow and where the feeding of a cat, the frying of a kidney, usurp the space normally commanded by plot. It has a nymph too – Calypso.

Ruari Owen has accepted a substantial redundancy payment and no longer works in children's television. He is now a freelance music critic.

Frederic Raphael

Brief notes on Kafka in Wonderland

Idris Parry's introduction to the Penguin edition of *The Trial* is interestingly reticent in one way, oddly assertive in another: 'Kafka must have come to [Max] Brod's that evening with a rare feeling of confidence. He had brought with him the manuscript of his first book…' The assertion that Kafka was 'confident', when it is well known that he later ordered his friend, Max Brod, to burn his manuscripts, seems recklessly 'imaginative'. Parry's reticence is announced by the flagrant repression of the word 'Jew'. He elects to find the source of *The Trial* in Kafka's relations with Felice Bauer and with her supplanting friend, Grete Bloch. (A Herr Block, a businessman like Kafka's *menschlich* father, cf also Portnoy snr, features in the novel.) It is as if Parry would have us believe that Kafka was never 'on trial', never felt himself under judicial scrutiny, except when it came to his painful engagement to Felice.

Academically averse to the obvious, Parry represses the truth: Jewjewjewjewjewjewjewjewjewjew is the implicit theme of the whole work, even if the work is not a whole.

'Someone must have made a false accusation against Josef K.' The world-political significance of unwarranted arrest is often said to have accumulated after Kafka's book, quite as if *déraison d'état* began only with totalitarianism. Was the previous history of the German-speaking and of the Hapsburg worlds, before 1914, both rational and just? What Kafka described was the present no less than the future. No one, it has been said, who did not live in Hapsburg Prague can ever fully understand the miasmic mixture of bureaucratic officiousness and legalised corruption which instructed Kafka. Vaclav Havel was accused of perpetuating the systematic disillusion which he himself has denounced.

There is never any escape from the whippers whom Josef K discovers at work on their own colleagues. Sadism is fun; the pleasure-principle outranks and outlives all ideologies. Even after 50 years, Heinrich Heine never forgot being caned by Padre Dickerescheit (what names reality comes up with!), after other pupils at the Franciscan school had mockingly impersonated their Jewish classmate: to be mocked is to be responsible for disorder. The victim is stigmatised for being victimised. Heine took the half-open door into Christianity which Josef K declines to enter when the cathedral verger offers it to him.

The dreaminess of *The Trial* is established at once, with the entrance of the arresting 'warders' into Josef K's bedroom. It will be declared, most blatantly, in the scene where the crowd in the 'courtroom' are seen to have cushions on top of their heads to prevent them being chapped by the ceiling. As in Arthur Schnitzler's *Traumnovelle*, we are introduced into an oneiric world, world as dream/reality. Does our greatest mistake with regard to Freud perhaps lie (ah the omnipresent duplicity of 'lies'!) in thinking that he made a severe (severing) distinction between dream and reality? The solipsist – who Wittgenstein said was, in some ways, right – reconciles them: his life is a fabrication, or fabulation, just as our dreams are. In Richard Rorty's sense the dream language redescribes the waking state, and vice versa.

It is tempting to say that Freud thought dreaming more real. The tenacious claim on our attention of Schnitzler's *Traumnovelle* does not derive from its plausibility, but rather from its conflation of dream and life. When, at the end of his novel, Kafka's alter ego realises that he is to die 'like a dog', it no longer matters whether he is dreaming this or whether it is 'really' about to happen. He is no better served in fantasy than in truth, or vice versa.

In *Une tragédie française*, Tzvetan Todorov tells the true story of the arrest of Jews in the town of St Amand, in the Cher, in June 1944. The arrested men and women had had no part in the 'crime' of killing Miliciens for which they were almost all to be executed. During the arrests, one man tried to hide. The Milicien in charge said, 'Il faut l'attacher, ce chien-là, car il se sauvera'. (Sartre would later call anti-Communists 'chiens'.) When Colonel Fernand Bernheim, a veteran of 76, was arrested, he said, 'Il faut que vous soyez tombés bien bas pour venir m'arrêter.' He had done nothing wrong, but they killed him too, like a dog.

* * *

On p 101 of *The Trial*, we read:

> It was eleven o'clock, he had wasted two hours dreaming... All the same, the time had not been completely lost; he had taken a decision which could prove valuable.

Freud interprets dreams in the light of reality; Kafka reverses the process (*The Trial* is translated into French as 'Le Procès', not an event but a continuum). The alienated jewjewjewjewjewjew cannot share the public world, in which he is always accused: although alone, he is not a singular defendant. If, in his inner being, he knows himself innocent and 'mistakenly' indicted, he is soon sure that he will be convicted. In court he says:

> What has happened to me... represents of course only one individual case, and as such it is not very important, since I do not take it too seriously, *but it's typical of the proceedings instituted against many people.* I speak here for those, not for myself. (p 33, my emphasis).

Note the definitive distinction between being bullied and being persecuted. Often the things seem to converge, but the difference is this: the individual victim is (however unjustly or cruelly) bullied as himself; those who are persecuted are merely instances. Josef K has generalised experiences but no specific history (apart from having an uncle). His conduct may be correct (he is capable, prudish, slightly priggish) but we have no idea of what might justly be alleged against him, only of the unspoken, and inescapable, original sin: jewjewjewjew. Cf Cavafy's 'you shall not find other places': as Josef K is persecuted in the nameless city (Prague), so will he be persecuted in the whole world.

The comedy of *The Trial* – Kafka is said to have laughed so much, when reading it aloud, that he could not continue – alerts us both to the absurdity of inquisition and to the grotesqueness of a world 'order' based on the fundamental lie which is, but cannot be said to be, Christianity. By it all Jews are defined, regardless, as criminals. Even those who seem to escape – like Heine? – can expect, one day, to encounter a higher tribunal (the Last Judgment?). What is false about what has been said about Josef K is the true measure of the civilisation in which he lives and which, with his crassly conformist Bohemianism, the painter Titorelli repeatedly embellishes and endorses (Art too is a department of the legal system).

The wanton girls, or nymphets, who frolic in the painter's apartment are sweetly paralleled in Schnitzler's *Traumnovelle*, where a shameless young girl is prostituted by her supposed guardian. The 'hero' of Schnitzler's novella may not come to the same savage end as Josef K, but he too is 'tried', by a corrupt, or libertine, court, although he has done nothing wrong and barely escapes with his life. He is an outsider who seeks to question the validity of those who sit in judgment on him. 'Hep hep' [an acronym for Hierosylema est Perdita], anti-Semitic fraternities used to shout after Jewish students: 'Gotcha!' so to speak. First the verdict, then the trial: 'Mitteleuropa Through the Looking Glass.' The isolation of the victim is procured by what Rakosi, that vengeful post-Hapsburg (Jewish) Stalinist, called 'salami tactics'. The scapegoat's separation from others facilitates his humiliation and murder. The loss of solidarity, the illusion of being uniquely despicable, prepares the victim for immolation. The victim has to nod as he is sacrificed.

After Josef K came Victor K(lemperer) whose meticulous diaries of his years of legal persecution, as the Jewish husband of a Gentile wife, are an undreamed version of *The Trial*, with a 'happier', even more ironic conclusion: first a liberal agnostic, then an exquisitely humiliated victim, finally he became an East German professor, acquiescent in Stalinism. The dream is a joke is reality is not a joke.

The latest volume of Frederic Raphael's ongoing memoirs, *Personal Terms*, was published by Carcanet in 2013. This piece first appeared in Issue 5 of *Areté*.

Craig Raine

Motley

1

The stream with its flags
streams like a tethered flag.
The perfect disguise.

2

Delapidated Venice,
chic shabby, tipsy churches,
mottled marbles underfoot,
nothing intact, its stuccos staccato:
O Horatio, what a falling off was here…

5

The plane tree's d.p.m.

Troops on leave
in identical jigsaws.

On Riva degli Schiavoni,
Panama hats piled up like Pringles.

4

Light on the water,
sunlight on the canal
this haute couture camouflage
of watered silk, this eau de nil,
these shadowed greens.

6

The long road patched
like a pair of jeans
making its way
to allotments
patched like a pair of jeans.

7

Funny thing, humour.
In Sterne, we study it.
To find out why it was funny once.
The half-life of jokes.

3

The dictionary's identity parade
of suspect suspects.

10

(For example, 'fool'.
Very deceptive.)

8

Funny word, ‘funny’.
Pretty peculiar.
Peculiar word, ‘pretty’. Very.

9

My father’s hands before he died.
Cartographic. Boundaries. Edges.
Uncertain of the destination,
or what was sea
and which was land.
Or what the pigment meant.
He was the map.
And the map knew where it was going.

Our Bold

More Recycling: Eagleton's DIY Clichés

This is Terry Eagleton's first sentence in *How to Read Literature* (2013): **'Like clog dancing**, the art of analysing works of literature is almost dead on its feet.' This is Eagleton's second sentence in *How to Read a Poem* (2007): **'Like thatching or clog dancing,** literary criticism seems to be something of a dying art.' Are they related? Should we be told? There's a lot of incest and inbreeding here. We think 'a dying art' and 'dead on its feet' are clearly related too.

Good job this recycling was on the first page, otherwise we might not have noticed its thriftiness. Page two is where we usually give up.

Peter Leggatt

I

OPENING TO A SHORT STORY

If the eyes are the windows to the soul, as Plato says, then perhaps hands are the signposts, and GE's were immaculately manicured. As he entered the lecture theatre the white fingernails of his left shocked the black hide of a leather satchel, wherein his books, and rested there with a delicacy both fay and fell. The distals were ivory-bright, of a kind with the sharp teeth beneath thin lips and the limpid sclera around their pale, blue irides. These accents matched the prematurely white hair of a 57-year-old who used to smoke and drink heavily (a glass of whisky with the morning lecture, latterly replaced by a sinister glass of milk), and played against a naturally tan complexion. He stood about five foot ten, and walked a little mincingly – threateningly if you knew him, sympathetically if you knew him well – in black Armani jeans above practical, brown, soft-looking shoes. It was thus that he took the stage, eyes cast down but bright with power, and, upon reaching the centre, whisked paper, a glass, and a plastic beaker full of milk from the satchel, placing them on the lectern. He dropped the bag, and, as he did so, began to talk in a voice that stroked the theatre into silence, pitched no louder than it might have been at a table for two.

One of the two most intelligent people I have ever met, what mystified me about GE, and what I considered as I sat there and listened, was that his clinical examination of anything before him – his ability to dissect a poem with the white clarity those nails and teeth and eyes implied – did not prevent occasional, astonishing departures of perspective, as when he emailed my fellow, very straight, undergraduate, R, who had sensuous lips, and invited him over for 'tea and an exchange of bodily fluids'. It was as though he could look at everything with the eyes of a god including most, but not all, of himself.

INVENTORY

[Subjective but neither invented nor invalid. This catalogue was ascertained accurate at the time of one thing or another.]

Thus his apartment contained: the waxed wooden floors of the Fellows' rooms at Lord's; floor to ceiling bookshelves in the main room filled with elegant editions of all kinds; other rooms seemingly, I think, with little ladders or steps into spaces with ear-high ceilings, from which books for you to borrow would be procured with uncanny generosity by this severe, predatory critic; a metal desk in an annex of the main room, with a desktop computer, arrays of papers and a rubber plant; photographs on the walls of what I thought may have been Minoan statues; a circular steel table with four steel chairs; a small kitchen, from which tea would be offered and produced that, perhaps due to the Cambridge water, would remain too hot or too distracting to drink during the hour or half-hour supervisions, and left unfinished would then add to the embarrassment of the student who had just been critically burned; a framed note written by Tennyson next the kitchen door; a replica of Keats's death mask hanging in an alcove of the bookcase, from when, I think, either the British Museum or the Keats-Shelley House in Rome used to sell them; in the shelf of the alcove, a tiny sculpture of a man the height of a five-pence piece beneath a tree the height of a 50-pence piece, all on a flocked-grass diorama about a foot in diameter and protected (or artistically incorporated) beneath a glass hemisphere, an artwork I think was called 'The Prophet', but it might have been 'The Prophecy'; a quantity of cats (precise number uncertain, possibly three) including the kitten Dolores, who lived in a cardboard box when I met her, and to whom GE would sometimes address comments during a supervision; pine steps to a small French window and roof patio, with a tomato plant growing just outside the door; a collection of records, mainly classical, and a record player; a treadmill (I'm not sure if I've imagined this, but I'm pretty sure I saw it there once at a party); a smell of dried tea.

PLAYSCRIPT

The scene is GE's apartment, set with sundry items selected from inventory (see above). GE is sitting in a metal chair at a round metal table drinking tea – the herbal smell should waft to the audience. After a pause, he moves to the back of the stage and opens the curtains to his tomato garden.

CURTAINS UP

A knock at the door

GE: Come iiin? (*sing-song tone*)

Enter PL

PL: (…)

GE: Well?

PL: Well, er, good morning.

GE: (…) Morning to you. Would you like some tea?

PL: Er, yes please.

GE: Have a seat.

(PL sits. GE exits stage right into the kitchen; PL looks around, and shuffles his, er, papers. At this point the actor playing PL must convey that PL is unsettled by the curtness of GE's welcome.)

GE: (*From stage right*) Milk?

PL: Yes please.

GE: Sugar?

PL: No thanks. (…) Sweets for the sweet, as they say.

GE: (…)

(GE *returns with extremely hot tea. It is at that stage of heat where it is so fucking hot that there is practically no steam – just a shimmer above the mug*)

Careful, it's hot. (*Spoken dangerously*)

PL: Thanks. (*Looks confused*)

GE: So, I read your notes for this dissertation idea. It certainly sounds possible. You want to write on Beckett's play, *Play*. Fine. There are a few things you must read, particularly interesting regarding repetition, since the play repeats itself – though perhaps with slight differences – at the middle point. First is Beckett's monograph on Proust, if you haven't read it already.

(*PL, who has taken up pen and paper, does not write this down, indicating that he has read it, a fact which the actor playing PL must convey using his face that PL is hopelessly keen to show. GE, however, is only glancing at him sidelong occasionally throughout this scene, except when he explains something*)

The next is – I am so sick of this notion of 'play' but not everyone is, so I suppose you ought at least to know about it – an essay called 'Structure, Sign and Play in the Human Sciences' in Jacques Derrida's *Writing and Difference*. Then, for the theatrical elements, read Meyerhold's originally-titled book *Meyerhold on Theatre*, and *Über das Marionettentheater* by Heinrich von Kleist. Have you –

PL: (*Struggling to keep up with the writing*) – Sorry G–, could you possibly slow down a little and tell me the title of the last one again?

GE: Ah, sorry. Yes, it's *Über* (…) *das* (…) *Marionettentheater*. It's a short book about puppet theatre and the limits of human gracefulness. It might be quite hard to find, but I imagine it ought to be in Lord's Library. Otherwise I'm afraid you will have to go to the UL, in which case my condolences. (*PL laughs while writing*) (...) O-Kayee?

PL: (...) Yup.

GE: OK. Also, Edward Gordon Craig, *On the Art of the Theatre*. That has some quite fascinating passages on asking impossible demands of actors, or the fact that many such ordinary demands are quite impossible. OK. You've read *Beyond the Pleasure Principle*?

PL: Um, yes.

GE: Right, well as you know that deals largely with repetition, and repetition-compulsion, and whether or not the characters in *Play* are compelled to repeat, or to what extent, is kind of a pivotal question. There is a difference between the compulsion to repeat and repeating compulsively. There is a difference (*more pensively, lifting finger to air*) (...) between the compulsion to repeat (...) and repeating compulsively. Take a smoker. He repeats the action of smoking a cigarette compulsively, but his compulsion is to smoke, not repetition itself. In the case of the obsessive-compulsive, on the other hand, who feels he must perform each action twice or a number of times, the compulsion might then be said to be the repetition, not the action. Freud, crucially, doesn't distinguish between the two phenomena, so whilst he names this new drive he concocts 'repetition-compulsion', it is not in fact a particularly useful name, because the compulsion, for example, to relive war trauma is due to a drive to attempt psychically to sort it out, not to a drive for repetition. Jonathan Lear approaches this point – in fact, add this to your list, it's a book called *Happiness Death and the Remainder of Life*. In fact, you can have my coffee. (*GE gets up*) Copy.

PL: Oh, that's very kind G – (...)

(*GE has got up from the table and moved into another room, through door at back of stage*)

(...)

(*He returns, holding the book delicately*)

GE: Here it is.

PL: Brilliant, thank you. Is it named after that Solon moral – call no man happy until he is dead?

At this point, the actor playing GE is impassive, and the actor playing PL must register to the audience using his face and body (optional) that he cannot tell whether GE has heard him, knows Solon, or doesn't know it (which the actor playing PL must simultaneously register using his face and body (optional) that he would find surprising), whilst continually suggesting concentration and deference to GE.

GE: So, bring that back when you're done with it.

PL: I will.

GE: Um um um um (...) Tut tut ti tum (...) Obviously read all of Beckett's plays if you haven't done so already. James Knowlson's lamentably-titled biography, *Damned to Fame*. It's an awful brick of a book but thorough, so written only for this kind of thing unless you are also a masochist for a crap prose style. Ruby Cohn's stuff is crap but celebrated. I suppose you have to at least look at *Just Play*, though it won't I doubt be as helpful as the title might suggest. Beckett's *Murphy* is a fun read, as are the four novellas, so look at those if you haven't already, but I wouldn't bother too much at this point with the other novels, novellas, or the trilogy. Your French leaves a little to be desired, as we discovered reading Flaubert together, didn't we?

PL: Ha, yes I'm afraid so.

GE: Right. Well in that case I think that will do you pretty well for now. Do you have any more questions?

PL: Um, no I don't think so. I'll look forward very much to reading all this stuff.

PL stands up, with papers and book. At this point, a cat emerges from the window onto the tomato garden upstage, and walks down stage right past the table.

GE: Good.

(*GE sees the cat. His face lights up and voice heightens to the pitch that some people use to talk to animals. It is surprising coming from him*)

(*Makes kissing noises*) HellO Dolores. (*Makes kissing noises*) *You* speak excellent French, don't you?

(*PL laughs, GE does not*)

GE: Yes, you do.

PL: Haha. I also wanted to ask you, G–, just before I go, whether you are working on anything at the moment?

GE: Oh, I'm writing up some of my lectures. (…) No doubt for a book that no one will read.

PL: (*laughs, but nervous*) Well I certainly will.

GE: Yes, well, perhaps all is not totally lost. (…) OKayyy?

PL: (*slightly nervous again, but purposeful*) Great, thanks so much G–. I was also wondering (…) I don't know whether you will be free, but I managed to get two tickets to see the Beckett that's on at the Fitzpatrick. It's *Endgame*, I think. I don't know whether it will be any good, but it's on on Sunday if you'd like to come, and maybe go for a drink afterward somewhere.

GE: (*Not looking up*) Sounds good. Let's go.

PL: OK great, thanks G–! See you on Sunday.

GE: OK then. (…) Byee.

(*PL looks nervously at his undrunk tea, then walks swiftly out by stage right, shutting the door carefully. GE places his pen onto the pad on the desk. He stands up, and takes PL's tea and his own (half-finished) into the kitchen.*)

Note on playscript

The manuscript ends here. As this is the end of the page, it is unclear whether there is supposed to be more of the play or whether that is it. The audience is left gratified and hopeful but nonetheless slightly puzzled. If this response has not been achieved the performance must be deemed a failure and should begin again.

RECIPE FOR SEDUCTION

Serves two

Ingredients

½ oz butter

½ tbsp sunflower oil

1 small chicken

4 streaky rashers bacon

4 small shallots

100g button mushrooms

½ oz plain flour

150ml chicken stock

150ml Wednesday's claret

1 large clove garlic, crushed

Salt and black pepper

2 tbsp chopped parsley to garnish
200g baby carrots
200g small potatoes
Panache
Sprezzatura

2 bananas
3 tbsp brown sugar
Olive oil
Rum
Vanilla ice-cream

Method

1. Melt butter with oil in casserole. Add chicken and cook for twelve min until brown. Lift out, leave to drain on tea towel (remember to buy more paper towels).

2. Add bacon, shallots, mushrooms, and cook over high heat, stirring until golden brown (well, it says 'golden brown', but does bacon ever really go 'golden brown'?).

3. Remove mixture and leave to drain on tea towel.

4. Add flour to pan, cook for five min until browned, then gradually stir in wine and stock.

5. Return chicken, bacon et al to casserole and add panache, garlic, salt and pepper. Bring to boil, cover, and cook at 190 °C for 45 min until tender.

6. Open bottle claret.

7. Invite the student to an ambiguously peopled and intentioned 'light supper' at your flat, at which, it smoothly and (one hopes) unrufflingly transpires, they are the sole guest.

8. Open door wearing black Armani jeans and black collarless shirt of light linen, suggesting casual, undecorated, and certainly undesigned elegance.

9. Ensure the main room is lit by two lamps, one floor one table, but that the lighting in the other rooms (kitchen especially) should shine at least a little more brightly and thus beckoningly, hinting at the access therein of further hallows, whilst simultaneously creating a shrouded and privileged atmosphere for the supper itself. Mahler plays lightly in the background, sinuously punctuated by the sizzle of *coq au vin*, or some-such somewhat sophisticated performance. In all the aforementioned, it is important not to overcook whilst attempting the desired effect.

10. Offer drink, pouring claret briskly (cf Samuel Johnson, possibly quoting this[1]), gesture at nuts on metal table, and immediately disappear into kitchen. This is both to suggest casualness, almost as apology for the fact that your guest is your sole guest, and an attempt to create a relaxed (but nonetheless decorous) atmosphere. Nevertheless the guest is not expected to feel wholly at home, since whilst this immediate disappearance and the conversation continued shoutingly from the kitchen does allow them to take in the situation, light, wine etcetera more carefully without the pressure of observation, it is still disquieting to be immediately eschewed by one's host in this manner and thus couples the effect of said relaxed tone with the seductive insult of the lack of presence, immediately putting the evening ever so slightly out of joint and creating a space for the play of the unexpected. The student should feel that action has been taken to put him at ease without actually feeling overmuch easy.

11. After student takes his seat at round metal table, ask solicitously (but still with the threat of criticism) whether he has any dietary requirements and whether *coq au vin* (or whatever it happens to be) will be 'adequate'. Slight mockery can enter the tone here, but which is nevertheless not entirely immodest since it is also gauged to suggest the over-sophistication of the host, hinting further (with the implication of social necessity but not necessarily sincerity) that *coq au vin* might not be something everyone can appreciate.

[1] 'Claret is a drink for boys, port is a drink for men, but he who aspires to be a hero must drink brandy.'

12. Allow the guest to sit at the table for a few moments before bringing out further nuts, returning to the kitchen, and initiating a little more raised and rather strained conversation. These continual disappearances of the host and interlocutor are also designed to achieve an odd 'behind the wizard's curtain' effect of mysterious preparation, continuing the mystery of the supervisor adopting his homely role, and thus attempting to preserve the bridge of unfamiliarity and curiosity that makes seduction most uncertain, noncommittal and dangerous.

13. Allow guest to steep for one minute, then shoutingly and summarily ask him for a hand. The purpose of this is multifold, designed a) to unsettle him once again, both physically and psychologically, since he has but sat down when he is asked to get back up, whilst also b) tacitly suggesting that (despite the fact he has not yet really been given a chance) he ought to have offered to help in the kitchen already. This and the other requests/instructions that follow are themselves part of a recipe for retaining an element of command, although it is a soft command since the host has also clearly gone to some trouble to prepare the meal and, by what is seeming to become a potentially unexpected date, 'put himself out there.' It is therefore an essay to retain the dignity of the supervisor despite the fact that he is clearly enamoured with the student, and to indicate (with a becoming bashfulness) tenderness through strictness, in the way that a father feels he ought to be all the more strict with the child he loves so fiercely that attempting any other behaviour would be to expose himself and result in an effusion of affectionate, spoiling, and self-demeaning attentions. The instructions also provide c) conversation on a practical level, since it is always better to be doing something on a date to avoid the awkwardness of acknowledging that it is a date, and d) permit conversation without eye-contact, which you are more strict about than the student, thereby enabling you to advertise yourself whilst remaining apparently passive and demure. Pressure at this stage would be a mistake, and the flattery of attentions and preparations must needs be balanced by some coldness and lightness of touch.

14. Simmer carrots and small potatoes in water for ten minutes on medium heat. Add salt and/or a dash of olive oil as desired.

15. Is the *coq au vin* quite cooked? Hm – you don't want the wine and blood to tart.

16. When done, take plates to table with student and bring the bottle

over, refilling (yes, already) your glass, *then* his.

17. Sit down and begin eating forthwith, eschewing (the absurdities of) courteous invitation to start. This is both to indicate your more direct and pragmatic approach and to suggest the enclave commensurate with the fact that both of you recognise such fripperies as fripperies, which, between men of a certain intellectual calibre, can be dispensed with. Such a stoicism is, it may be acknowledged, at odds with the delicacy of the dish and the evening, but the fucking that dare not speak its name need not be fancified.

18. 'So, G–, what have you been up to today?' L should now ask into the silence. Reply along non-committal, world-weary lines before opening up upon something that actually was quite interesting – e.g. 'Oh, just trying to redeem the same unforgivables in class and to find the time to work my lectures into a book that no one will read' – then hurriedly, before any awkward interjection from L that he might read it, or similar commiseration – 'Ah, but actually, today I was in the tea rooms of the University Library having tea with FE, which is where all the work gets done anyway, discussing hiring a new Fellow from Princeton who might end up teaching you, and who I'm interviewing on Wednesday.' 'Do you think he'll survive?' 'Yes I imagine he will actually, he's a very studious Renaissance scholar doing interesting work on – wait for it – tickling.' 'Tickling?' 'Tickling and 'the sense of touch' in sixteenth-century England. It's rather interesting – have you read Adam Phillips, his book called I think *Kissing, tickling and being bored*?' 'I haven't, but I do know that pattern of romance and I know Phillips.' 'Hm. Yes well it's the only book that seems interested in tickling, and this new candidate has some very interesting and promising things to say on the strange topic. But *you* L–, what have you been up to today?' By changing the topic here, or in this general manner, suggest that you have more to say (and which is perhaps more interesting than L's conversation, playing down any hint of your infatuation), but that you are demurely waiting for him to spark *your* interest before you open up on further discourse. Something of the suggestion that you are almost bored, it occurs to you, often in fact leads better into kissing then, perhaps, tickling; with the hope things don't come full circle.

19. A certain amount of demure badinage from beautiful – and really quite clever – L should be expected here. We hope the claret is up to the expectations of the man from Eton. Do they teach that there these days?

20. Events should flow smoothly from this point. If not, add one glass claret every ten minutes until desired effects transpire.

21. Segue into kitchen. Peel two bananas, then slice into halves lengthwise. Tell L to add three tablespoons brown sugar to pan on medium heat. Once melted but not smoking, add three drops olive oil and stir by moving the pan. Add bananas. Turn up heat incredibly high, all of a sudden, and pass L bottle of rum. Instruct to flambé, from close behind him. A certain amount of physical contact is at this point encouraged, and certainly also coy chastisement at any failures of L.

22. A sense of blissful confusion should at this point arise in both parties, amongst the flames on the stove, the wine's lulling hold, the smell and vapour of the melting sugar, and the excitement of two normally intelligent and composed but at this point free and glistening faces in the flashing of the firelight. If L fails to flambé successfully proceed to step (25). If he succeeds, continue thus –

23. Add one scoop vanilla ice cream to plates and serve.

24. Eat bananas on sofa.

25. Apply sherry. At this point, the Mahler should have ended and the confused and pleasantly confusing sound of the record player frictively repeating the inner rim of the record should resonate in the warm room, escaping just outside the windows into the blackest, windy Cambridge night.

26. Kissing/tickling (?)

DISCLAIMER

All of the events and persons in this account are fictional. None of the events or persons here described are based on others, real or fictitious. GE, a week or two following the events already set down, did not have a heart attack followed by a major stroke. He did not have a stroke of luck, he did not stroke another person, did not practice his stroke on a court or a green and he did not swim or row. He did not have a stroke of genius and did not strike a blow with fists or other implements. He did not arrive, depart or remain on the stroke of any clock's strike, pistons did not travel, no two-stroke engines or any others fired or misfired. He certainly did not practise the strokes of his pen, stay out in the sun too long, or use the word 'stroke' so repeatedly that it lost all meaning and sense apophatically – stroke – aphasiatically. What particularly did not happen was that he was not walking on the path behind Lord's at the stroke of eleven when he felt a great pain in his chest, and telephoned his doctor who told him not to worry about anything and to book an appointment in the next few days. He did not then suffer from continued chest pain throughout the night, and by a stroke of luck manage to call a friend to see him minutes before he suffered a major heart attack and collapsed, to be found on her arrival. She did not stroke his hand in the ambulance, he did not appear to make a recovery in hospital the following afternoon and describe himself as feeling rather 'half-hearted'. I was not, at around this time, waiting at his door for our next supervision. In the late afternoon the anti-coagulants administered did not cause him to have a major apoplexy, cerebrovascular accident, cerebral infarct, necrosis of brain tissue due to an arterial thrombosis, embolism, haematoma, intra-axial haemorrhage, aneurysm, whatever you want to call it. He did not have a stroke –

L did not hear about this from the pompous college chaplain the next morning, when she leaned out of her window and asked, as he walked through the courtyard, if he knew what had happened to GE. L did not momentarily and inexplicably feel as though he was in trouble. He surely was able to help thinking how fustian she was when she did not say 'I mean, fuck the other fellows and the mathematicians, GE is Lord's brightest light', as though it were what GE needed or deserved at that time to have his intelligence praised. L did not hear more about it from his replacement supervisor SA three days later, who had not been to see GE in hospital, and who did not recount through tears that he was in a wheelchair, right-side paralysed and unable to speak, only to make the sound 'ti'...except for at one moment when he had looked at her in the eyes and stated 'It's a nightmare'. She did not later cry, the week after that, when GE was not improved and L mentioned that his neurologist parent said that the most substantial recovery from stroke happens in the first two weeks. She, it is certain, did not later try to seduce L after drinks (when in sadness he led her on) with a walk in the Fellows' garden, a conversation about Wittgenstein, and an invitation to join her in a hollow bush which, finding it a close and darkened place, L did not exit swiftly and probably abruptly.

Symbols did not, at this point, begin to take on a significance that they had not possessed before. L did not wonder at some of the statements made in his last supervision, pondering (as much as he could ponder in his melancholy state) the phrase 'call no man happy until he is dead' whilst leafing through GE's copy of *Happiness, Death, and the Remainder of Life*. GE's note on the epigram from Kafka, 'Human nature, essentially changeable, unstable as the dust, can endure no restraint', did not read '*is* dust unstable?', and L did not wonder further at repetitions, repetition-compulsions, repetitions, and at the crowded realisation that GE's speech – which consisted of the sound 'ti' spoken repeatedly, but with all the intonations and addenda of normal conversation – was neither compelled repetition nor repeated compulsively. If it was at all, which it wasn't, it would have been, rather, impelled language, immured in repetition. L did not find, in the library copy of Ruby Cohn's *Just Play*, GE's handwritten annotations, carefully rubbed out, perhaps from many years ago, making a ghostly palimpsest of erudition and erasure. Things did not, at this point, take on a significance that they had not possessed before. He did not have a stroke. Reader assumes full responsibility. Other restrictions may apply.

THE ANATOMY OF MELANCHOLY

As a bird buildeth his nest, so doth a man make his dreams, as from many divers particulars and mixed elements, which that he comes across in waking, as faces, actions, settings, feelings, yet all most often transmuted out of their first place and disposition. Thus it is proved, out of Aristotle, that man's dreams do not come to him from something exterior, but are formed of that part he has amassed within, and though in his sleeping invention he may seem to make something new out of the matter, yet it derives from knowledge precedent to his dreaming.

And, like as to the ship of Theseus that Plato saith, there is not one part that doth determine his dream to be a nightmare, but, to say the same, many conditions sufficient and none necessary, and hence there may be in a nightmare, but none for certain, any of the following: helplessness; paralysis; guiltiness; anxiousness; being possessed with a notion of repetition ineluctable; being possessed with a notion that events, actions etcetera occur to him overfast/overslow/both fast and slow in a single instance; dispossession of the faculty to speak his native language/to speak those other languages of which he hath knowledge/to understand the language of others and to find the good responses that a situation merits; loss of confidence in his station or convictions; sudden loss of the power of to make noise/of movement; and often loss of what is named, out of Scaliger, the 'senses of locomotion'. In addition there may manifest the sudden expansion/diminution/expansion and diminution simultaneous of objects individual or of space in sum; sometimes horrible feelings of a wonder that doth not uplift but rather makes timid his person; the sensation of knowledge unable to place as with, like they say, a 'word on the end of the tongue'; distrust; distrust of his feelings (amongst which distrust); the impression of a disgusting cleanliness, or a repulsive dirtiness; hopelessness; a notion that he is dead or no longer living.

Further, the nightmare doth not restrict itself to sleep alone, but yet there may be in a man's rising hours all of the attributes that doth construct and attend malicious dreams in sleep. One part which might be approved a nightmare is like as to the appearance of ghosts, by which I refer to nothing supernatural (whereof I do treat in the proper place) but to the mistaken apprehension of someone well beknownst to the melancholic, and often the person who means the cause of a melancholy illness. So it is when a child seems to espy his mother in the market but, making to her, finds when she turns that she is not that woman but yet another, strange and not familiar to him. In great grief and after loss in particular a man can espy those whom he has loved, not merely in the whole figure – as a man turning a corner of the cloisters in his college – but also by one part, or a part of a part thereof, in actions, manners etcetera, as in a shuffling of papers or the accent of another man's walk.

And there is a second waking symptom that hath all the attributes of the diminution of perspective forementioned. Thus, waking and half-unable to move or speak in the early morning, briefly unknowing as to how he arrived in that situation, and, it has been much observed, especially if he occupies a close room on the ground, the world entire may seem to a grown man of but ill and small consequence, as though it were the house that children have for dolls. Thus it is that, departing from sleep and finding oneself in a chair, stiff in limbs and some extremities, the world may seem mute and intransigent – as in nightmares – and especially small. Then his books are but the books of a doll's house, being short, barely scrutable, and seeming written as a pleasing jest for eyes larger and more seeing than his own; so his pictures are the pictures of the doll's house, in their rudeness of form, their base commemoration and parochial hand; his television is a total nightmare, of epileptic static; his furniture is brittle; the light is somewhat off, his face and yours sfumato shadows, miniscule particles on the surface of eternal night that swathes or swaddles this doll's house and examines it vastly, with little interest. It barely moves a thought, and he finds from his chair that it is of wooden and childish consequence.

ABOUT THE AUTHOR

GE sits in his wheelchair. His manner is the same; brusque, difficult, witted, and a cat roves the ground-floor room he has been moved into. He is the author-function of this story, finishing sentences with witticisms, ending phrases slow to come as a son does his father's slowing speech, and as that father did his father's before in a course running backward of utterances shared and completed. He makes ironic remarks on the tone, decides that 'the fucking that dare not…' is more apposite than 'love', notes with querying lines in the margins, provides a quotation here, corrects a reference there, and impels the writing. He is talked about at dinners and at drinks, his jokes aired there, miles and times away.

His old apartment must be empty now, but he writes this story from his past placement of pictures on the walls, of cats moving into cardboard boxes, and from an auction chair at a sale of poetic letters. This is still being written from my wheelchair, letter by letter on the keyboard with a finger of my left hand, and even though writing words is an impossibility, yet I described himself as above, invented a love affair, allowed some details here and there, and knew that narratives must happen in the past.

CRITICAL REVIEW OF THE STORY

Leggatt's story ' / ' exhibits the emotional and formal struggle of writing about aphasia. On the one hand, the text seems to commiserate and empathise with the struggle of a man who cannot speak or conduct language, but inevitably this is done in words, and so the story has not only to negotiate the semantic problems of expressing linguistic deficit in language but must also face the ironies and guilt of writing decoratively/expressively about a man whose inability to express might seem flaunted by the very attempt to empathise with it artistically. In addition there is the perennial problem of tragic literature, which speaks about things that, we might want to say, are so appalling they ought to render us speechless. Creative utterances have particular taboos, for they can both appear to revel in events by artistic retelling and risk an insulting falsification of the story, since this creative use of language necessarily invokes a 'play' of possible meanings. Tragic literature is at once redemptive and cruel when it brings art that entertains from events it wants to recognise as the dire opposite of entertaining, and Leggatt's story renders (and possibly also attempts to negate) this empathic paradox; or he finds the story rending itself in the work's own formal code-switching.

This rendering or rending is most salient in the changes of generic form, a linguistic struggle which constitutes a textual dramatisation of the aphasiac's plight. The story is divided into labelled sections (e.g. 'Recipe', 'Playscript') with associated formal qualities, a series of shifts which enact the difficulty of trying to find a way to speak about speechlessness, as if each form in turn were found inadequate to narrate the story. As aphasia moves away from linguistic form yet sometimes remains within language, so Leggatt rejects the stylistic conditions of the short story within one, dispensing with what is explicitly this mode of writing in his opening. Yet the fact that '/' remains, nevertheless, a short story is also of significance, since this particular form seems fitting to map the content – language, and normal life, cut short. The story's abbreviation and the constant, constantly abbreviated use of differing forms within this larger one all serve formally to repeat the horrific abbreviation of one of the lives it concerns. The form itself, if you will, is made to stutter.

The event of the stroke itself appears (or fails to) in a passage marked 'Disclaimer', which deals with the problem of speaking about speechlessness (why isn't there 'writelessness'?) by refusing to do so affirmatively, whether by defining the incident apophatically or ironically. This passage is the pivot of the story, and the negative tone is a choice device. First, by denying the occurrence of the stroke, Leggatt achieves the pathos of a furious attempt to undo an event, to rewrite wishfully, and thus the tone of a passage ascribed the normally dulling conventions of a publishing caveat is made emotionally compelling. Second, writing in the negative circumnavigates a problem of writing about aphasia, providing a perennial reminder of the inequity of language to the job that is similar to the use of apophasis in religious writing to speak about God. Third, stating that something did not happen with enough insistence cannot help but bring to mind the opposite possibility, and we might even be led to wonder at the fictional status of the narrative itself and question whether these events might in fact really have occurred. If fiction is not fact, perhaps the insistence in a fictional account that something did not happen paradoxically suggests more firmly that it did.

The word 'stroke' is the subject of Leggatt's incessant punning in the same passage, which seems both to enact the horrible repetitions of aphasia after a stroke, and to highlight the seeming inconsequence of our lexical/ semantic choices versus the power they have to name, with grave differences of import, things in reality. The frivolity of the punning and its field of meaning are held beneath a single, terrible sense which crushes the possibility of wordplay where it applies. In this context Leggatt's title is a victory for his innovation, for '/', whilst translated implicitly by the context as the word 'stroke', is in fact a symbol that cannot be said, and thus Leggatt's title at least does formal obeisance to its subject matter. Whether or not we find it a strain to construe '/' as 'stroke', since that is largely a translation accorded in British English, is perhaps an issue, and we might also wonder whether Leggatt has missed a trick in that the symbol can also be used to bracket phonemic transcriptions of speech. '/' is also one of those lovely symbols which, like some words, describe or accommodate their own multivalent senses. Thus '/' is itself a single stroke of the pen, or the keyboard, whilst the relationship between each of its meanings, including that one, can be described by another of its senses: 'or', since '/' can mean a stroke of the pen/ or etc. '/' itself, then, describes the internal relations a symbol requires for punning, as the word 'play', for example, can describe the mechanical play (or freedom of movement) that the multivalent senses of that word itself permit. The function of '/' to mean 'or' also gives the story a title that embraces and suggests alternatives – of style, voice, person, and even the notion that the apoplectic stroke itself might not have happened. '/' is at once untranslatable, refuses to be linguistically enunciated and played with, yet suggests the very play of alternatives that structurally enable puns. Like the language of the aphasiac, it at once signifies nothing translatable and a plurality of possible meanings.

By containing the story's own analysis within it, and taking critical, exterior perspectives on the story within the story itself, Leggatt effaces and complicates the role and position of the narrator, dealing again with the topic of writelessness by attempting to render the story writerless. The changes of grammatical person throughout contribute to this endeavour, for the story begins in the first-person, moves to the tonally unpersonified voices of the 'Playscript', and finds the second-person and GE's free indirect speech in the 'Recipe'. This is followed by the largely third-person mode of the 'Disclaimer' before the prose retreats into the early seventeenth-century English that precedes the blurring of person/s in the section entitled 'About the Author'. It might, however, be said that the flow of the story's fictional narrative somewhat subsumes the critical project of formal struggle, since by incorporating the narrative break (GE's sudden end to language) or finding a form that it fits rather than breaks – the *short* story – Leggatt gives formal sense to an event which he simultaneously wants to say happened senselessly; gives formal structure to the collapse of structure, so whilst trying to avoid the imposition of meaning and language upon what is meaningless and unspeakable through stylistic form, in order to make the story function he seems unable to do away with the happy signification of its narrative genre. The move could perhaps be analysed as a Freudian 'covering-over' through narrative of what is in fact a site of trauma; using the story's abbreviation as a stylistic device naturalises that shortness, makes purposeful a real abbreviation that was wildly (and traumatically) unnatural and purposeless, and not just unintended but undesired.

Finally, by incorporating analysis into the story, Leggatt runs an enormous risk, since he both exposes himself to the accusation of critical arrogance or narcissism, and sets himself up for abject failure if his story does not support the weight of critical interpretation he puts upon it. By injecting a critical, self-aware voice into the critique itself Leggatt seems also to be attempting to head this off, but even this tactic is subject to the criticism that the prose becomes involved. Nevertheless, this reviewer maintains that '*/*' is worth reading, if only as the illustration of a grandiose but possibly failed staging of grief.

POST SCRIPT

When I last saw GE he was under the cloisters in Barrow's Court at the back of Lord's. There, Isaac Newton found the speed of sound by heavily stamping his foot and listening for the echo's return from the far wall; listening for his sound to come back to him.

GE made a small figure next the vast columns and desolate sandstone. He was with a therapist, climbing out of his wheelchair and, his left hand stretched back to hold the armrest, his back stooped and his knees bent, he was learning how to walk. Once he had managed to stand upright, he tentatively let go the chair and shuffled forward in his soft brown shoes, moving his left foot first, hardly off the ground, and the right after, not leaving the ground at all. This woman stood by him, to steady him if he stumbled.

It is not well to see a man who learned six or seven languages learning how to walk, repeating, repeating his steps. I waited at the far corner of the court, my bag on my shoulder, and watched this oddly silent scene – for GE's steps were strangely silent – until he had walked his ten yards, the wheelchair was brought back, and he sat. Then I began walking towards him, my footsteps echoing, and when I was a little way off gave my best 'Hello G–!' He greeted me with his same, cynical, trendily world-weary attitude, as though we were two who understood such fripperies of greeting as fripperies – two, perhaps, alone. As he would have in health, he clearly meant to keep the conversation brisk, so I told him what I was doing back at Cambridge, looking at a manuscript or something, asked something after his cats, and then told him I would let him go, or that I'm going to head off, or something equally, gallingly mundane – and yet impossible – and that I was very glad to see him. At parting he gave me his airy, singsong good-bye: a nulled, dreamt echo returning from the conversations we had made in health. 'Ti-tii'

Peter Leggatt graduated from Trinity College, Cambridge, in 2011, and now lives in London where he is trying to write a novel. '/' is his first short story.

Low C-flat, bread-and-butter note

Once upon a time, there were samplers of good prose, little snippets of perfection to promote emulation and imitation. No longer, alas, and therefore no obvious resting place for this elegant, perfectly-turned sentence from Adam Phillips's acknowledgements in *Becoming Freud: The Making of Psychoanalysis* (2014). He is thanking Ileene Smith, his editor at Yale: 'I'm not sure I could have written this book without the sense I have had that she got what I was wanting to do.'

Sam Gardiner

Two Poems

Cherish the Flexion

Joints triple hinged to swivel and flex,
move femur and tibia together, apart,
alive with arteries, blithe with nerves,
they brought her here by pure art, these knees,
from God knows how far away, or long ago,
and now pretend themselves freshly minted
instead of primeval, older than sin.

Rode white horses across dark seas, these joints,
climbed hills, skipped and danced, gathered potatoes,
rocked countless generation of children,
and now sit in an easy chair and eye me up,
twin patellae staring like small blind saucers.
Fleshed out in feelings, these knees of hers
are beautiful. Perfect for kneeling.

Pillion Riders

Changed my life, that Lambretta
I could not afford but had to have,
brought girls hours closer and places
nearer by miles, but did not help me
install a trophy bird on my pillion
to replace my usual basket full
of Dad's pigeons, all gutturally crooning
and yodelling, facing into the headwind
blowing hard from my destination.
Wrong kind of birds. I took them to
Rathfriland, Castlewellan, Poyntzpass,
and other places none of us wanted to be,
tossed them up, and timed them
while they circled unhampered through
a range of bearings until one rang true.
They then sped off and arrived home
long before I did. And used no petrol.

Sam Gardiner's latest book of poems, *The Morning After*, was published by Lagan Press in 2010.

Steven McGregor

Tension, Tension, Release

Percival loved getting his haircut. It only cost five bucks. It was away from the trailers and Corporal Ricardez. It was something to do.

'Anything to drink?' said Ibrahim the barber.

'Orange rain,' Percival said.

Ibrahim gave him a cold one.

'You know we don't have this back home.'

'Excellent flavor. Excellent quality and flavor,' said Ibrahim.

Percival sat in the barber's chair which was just an old office chair. He lit a menthol cigarette and offered one to Ibrahim. He accepted. On the television was a dark haired girl singing Arabic and twisting her hips.

'Who's the girl?' Percival said.

'Some gypsy.'

'She's hot.'

Ibrahim began with the electric clippers without even asking what to do. It was always the same. Take it all off. This was the pleasure of the barbershop: in a soft chair with his cigarette, his cold drink, and his rifle.

Vicky came in the barber shop and said, 'knew you'd be in here you bum.' He did a fist pound with Ibrahim who was holding the clippers. 'Can we smoke nargila?'

'Get Mohammed. He's sleeping.'

Vicky waited for a moment.

'Don't be embarrassed,' Percival said. 'Just go in there.'

Vicky went in the side room, behind the curtain. 'Wake up you bum,' he said to Mohammed. 'Let's smoke. Out here with these esteemed gentlemen.' He came back in the barber room. 'Who's the girl?'

'Some gypsy,' Percival said.

The haircut was over and Ibrahim took the money and put it in his coffee can and put the can in the safe where he kept it. Mohammed set up the nargila with his eyes mostly closed. He had shaggy black hair and a red fishnet shirt and fancy designer jeans and it was an act really because he was wise. He got a pass to work on the base after all. He was family with Ibrahim somehow.

'Apple okay?' Mohammed said about the tobacco.

'Yeah,' Percival said.

They sat in office chairs and smoked.

'Supposedly the mail's coming today,' Vicky said.

'I should be getting something,' Percival said.

'You always get something.'

Ibrahim and Mohammed were watching the gypsy.

Percival said, 'I spend all my money.'

'Is it more equipment for your studio?'

'No, this is something better.'

'What would you spend money on as a luxury?' Vicky asked Mohammed.

Mohammed just smiled without opening his mouth.

'You should have a nice gold necklace,' Ibrahim said. 'Every man needs a nice gold necklace and a ring. A ring with a stone maybe? Amber or a fine jewel. A ruby?'

'I'm a rapper. We only have diamonds,' Percival said. The apple smoke was very nice and it coated the inside of his mouth pleasingly and sweetly.

'Get your PT shit on,' said Corporal Ricardez, having silently opened the door somehow.

'Roger, Corporal,' Vicky said.

Percival didn't answer because he was blowing smoke.

'Meet by the trucks in five minutes,' Ricardez ordered and shut the door.

'What's with him?' asked Ibrahim.

'That's how he is. He's acting tough lately,' Percival said. He went with Vicky over to their trailer to change clothes and lock up their rifles. Sure enough the mail had come and it was on their beds. Percival held up a new package, a long cardboard box. It was heavy and narrow and packed tight so it wouldn't rattle. He wanted to save it for after PT but Vicky was guessing what it would be.

'You'll never guess,' Percival said. He pulled his uniform top and undershirt off, slipping them over his head in one motion, and threw them in the corner. They were still damp with sweat from the patrol hours before. He sat on the edge of his bed, with his elbows on his knees. His dogtags stuck to his wet chest.

'At least you don't have to clean the gun tonight,' Vicky said.

Percival said nothing. Vicky went outside.

'Some bullshit,' Percival said and he changed out of his ACU trousers into his nylon PT shorts. He unlaced his boots and put on his running shoes. He put on a PT shirt and sat down on his bed again, the thin mattress flattening under his weight.

There was a pounding on the outside wall and Vicky yelled, 'let's go.'

Percival tucked in his shirt with two hands and went out in the searing sun.

It was near dusk when the men returned to their rooms.

'Holy shit. You buy that?' Vicky said.

Percival gently lifted the body of the helicopter out of the case, feeling the tail warp until he freed it from the wire fasteners. In the front was the engine and the battery port, shielded by a black visor and blue plastic casing. The thin frame extended back with several metal rods to the tail propeller. '350QZ FastCat' was written along both sides.

Percival plugged in the battery by sliding it into place and when he nudged the twin sticks on the controller, the machine activated, tilting the rotor with an insect-like dexterity. There was a click and the three-foot rotor whirred.

'Fuck!' Vicky shouted moving back to the wall. 'Turn it off!'

Percival said, 'I can't.' He tried all the controller's switches, on, off. The machine was vibrating demonically, tapping its sleds on the floor. He kneeled beside it, curving his arm under the blades, his shirtsleeve flapping in the gust. With the tips of his fingers he managed to tug on the square, yellow battery and, as suddenly as it came to life, the motor died.

'It's a weapon,' Vicky said.

They placed it in the gravel road outside the concrete pad of trailers. Beyond them were the Humvees, combat parked with their front ends facing out, in a neat row. The sky was ruby like the inside of a grapefruit and Vicky said it looked like another sandstorm.

Hawkins and several men from the Scout platoon were throwing the football. They came over to watch. The helicopter waited on the gravel, as though a patient, well-trained bird of prey. Percival mashed the throttle upwards. The rotor became indistinct and with a kind of magic effort the machine lifted off the gravel rocks, hovering. It paused for a moment and then shot into the sky, straight up.

'Fuck me!' said Hawkins.

Then it began to corkscrew downwards. Percival reversed the levers on the controller and the helicopter straightened, swerving and then zooming higher. It was just like Percival had imagined. It was flying effortlessly and dipping and scoring across the violent sky.

Lieutenant Kerns and Sergeant Linden walked by on their way back from somewhere.

'Oh man, oh man,' Kerns said. 'The things Joe spends his money on.'

'He bought turntables last week, sir,' said Vicky.

'What for old records?'

'Yes, sir. Like a DJ.'

'For my studio, sir,' Percival said as he watched the helicopter. He made it circle around.

'What are you going to do with all this junk when we move to BP 152 next month?'

'Don't know, sir.'

'Let me try,' Vicky said.

But it turned over on its side and crashed in the rocks, not two feet from where it took off. The rotor beat against the ground and shattered with a dust cloud and the dying whine of the engine. The men stood motionless.

'That's it?' Kerns said.

Percival tried the controls but nothing responded. Vicky went forward and set the bird upright but still nothing.

'How much did that thing cost?' Kerns said. He seemed genuinely upset.

'I can't remember exactly, sir,' Percival said.

'A hundred bucks? Two-hundred bucks?'

Percival's face was plain like he had just woken up and not been dreaming. He raised his eyebrows and then walked to where the machine sat in the gravel. 'It was more than two-hundred,' he said. 'What else am I gonna do with the money?'

Steven McGregor was shortlisted for the Shiva Naipaul Memorial Prize in 2012 and 2013.

Oliver Reynolds

Poem

Autobiography

Oliver A
will not say

why Oliver F
was playing deaf

when Oliver R
went too far

Let Oliver S
mop up the mess

and so to bed
with Oliver Z

André Naffis-Sahely

Through the Rockies

for David Shook

It's my third sleepless dawn on the Zephyr
and I'm in Iowa. Outside my window,
a gopher tunnels out of its purgatory
and wobbles across the sugary snow.

Across the aisle, I watch Tanika crush
grains as pink as the sky, then take
a quick hit on her pipe. She's on the run…
Her six kids are somewhere in Indiana;

the last time she spoke to her mother,
the old woman shouted: 'No good
comes of breeding with niggers and spics',
meaning the fathers of Tanika's children.

'I wish I was in the Wizard of Oz',
Tanika mumbled as we sliced
through this American vastness.
Sometimes no-place is better than home.

Before long, the passion for sharing
spills into the air, like measles at school,
and everyone's mouths start to thaw.
The smile on the travelling salesman (a Nation

of Islam 5%er) depicts the weird joy we feel
when we survive one too many disasters.
The scars on his chest hug his green gang tattoos:
a lesson twice learned and thus never forgotten.

Everyone here has one foot in life and the other
in the future, or the past. Usually the past…
Jane, who looks and sounds like Jessica Lange,
reminisces about her time in the circus:

'It was the 70s, I was living in England,
and you really needed a union card
to get any work as an actress,'
so she spent five gruelling months

touring the continent on an elephant.
Her raw tongue licked the edge
of her jagged teeth: 'The dwarves
were the worst: mean, horny things…

one night, two of them tried to rape me,
but the bearded lady, my friend,
gave them a hiding they'll never forget!'
At Reno, Jane and the vets in their blue caps,

begin their week of blackjack and slots.
We slow down before Colorado
and during a stop munch our way
through Jane's special brownies;

Lenny, the conductor, plucks on his steel guitar
and yells, 'yo-delay, yo-delay, all aboard!'
Later, he hands me the day's newspaper:
Russia's invaded the Crimea, again.

If history occurs first as tragedy, then as farce,
then what shall we call this third act
we're trying so hard to survive in?
That evening, as we drew near to Chicago,

the passengers turned to face the horizon in unison,
and I watched a burst of dew crystallise
in the crisp, purple air, and each
molecule grow till it shone like a diamond.

'How pretty…', I'd thought, eyeing the burst
fade fast in the distance; sadly
all it meant, as Lenny later told me,
was that someone had just flushed the toilet.

André Naffis-Sahely was recently in residence at the MacDowell Foundation and took a trip on the California Zephyr.

Our Bold

2+2=0

In 'Dishing the Dirt' (*Spectator* 28 September 2013), Wynn Weldon was reviewing Christopher Reid's *Six Bad Poets*: 'The poem is divided into six parts of six chapters of six verses of six lines and reads as easily as Byron, the last line of each verse rhyming with the first of the next. The easiness of read – a hard thing to achieve – just about makes up for **this scarcity of rhyme, and by the end the nagging thought that satirical poems really ought to rhyme at the very least abab is thoroughly silenced.**'

Areté has been using the office abacus. That makes five rhymes per section, right?

Let's have a look. For example, these are the rhymes in Chapter 6, Section 3: 'coquettish'/'fetish'; 'goes'/'goose'; 'persuade'/'should'; 'more'/ 'pour'; 'Historical'/'memory stick'. You might wonder about that last rhyme but you'd be wrong: it's 'ric' and 'stick'. And it is a warning to the unwary that the rhymes are more ingenious than obvious. For example, in this section 3, 'coquettish' and 'fetish' also engrosses 'puppy-fattish', 'skittish', 'strict-ish', 'British'. Not necessarily in that order. Then there is 'your'/ 'door'/ 'war'/ 'more' / 'pour' / 'for'. Plus 'said' / 'sad' / 'persuade' / 'should' / 'shed' / and finally back to 'said'. What about 'memory stick'? 'Unstuck' / 'strike' / 'strict' / 'historical' / 'memory stick'. And 'goes'?: 'goes' / 'goose' / 'goes' / 'gaze' / 'girls'.

So, roughly 36 rhymes per section.

We can do it again with the opening section 1: 'poet' / 'apart' / 'poet' / 'start' / 'stoat' / 'port' / 'distrait'. And *this* set of rhymes is closely shadowed by another set of rhymes: 'Street' / 'stare at' / 'a start' / 'prat-' /

'straight' / 'pirate'. You can see that 'pirate' might rhyme with 'poet' just as easily as 'distrait' rhymes with 'poet'. Same section: 'jeans' / 'scenes' / 'gins' / 'ambitions' / 'apparitions' / 'monkeyshines'.

You get the idea. Not exactly rationing, is it?

By 13 December 2013, so little had changed, *Areté* wondered if the *Guardian*'s Ben Wilkinson wasn't Wynn Weldon using a pseudonym. Again, Reid's readability was praised and Byron invoked: 'The main thing to admire about *Six Bad Poets* is its readability. Eschewing the formalities of Byron and Pope that are the hallmarks of satirical verse, Reid pitches his lines between poetry and prose, though he is not beyond the occasionally brilliant end rhyme.' He cites 'prolix' and 'bollocks'.

We thought of dimwits and flummoxed.

Back Issues

Issue 1 T S Eliot – unpublished letters to James Joyce, Ezra Pound, Virginia Woolf & W B Yeats / Patrick Marber – Casting / New fiction by Ian McEwan and Peter Ho Davies / A prose poem by Harold Pinter / A la recherche du temps perdu – Craig Raine

Issue 2 William Golding – Scenes from a Life, an unpublished memoir / Julian Barnes and Rose Tremain – new fiction / Martin Amis and Ian McEwan on Borges / Christopher Logue on visiting Brecht

Issue 3 Boris Pasternak – Letters from a Marriage / Ralph Fiennes on acting Shakespeare / David Lodge – new fiction / Reviews by Frederic Raphael and Tilman Spengler / Christopher Reid – Eating Out, three poems

Issue 4 Martin Amis on literary criticism / Adam Thorpe – Towards a Little Theatre / James Fenton – seven songs / Colin Matthews – Diary of a Composition

Issue 5 Scenes from Harold Pinter's screenplay of Lolita / an interview with David Lodge / Blake Morrison on song lyrics / reportage by Peter Foster and Dorothy Gallagher

Issue 6 Christopher Logue – All Day Permanent Red, new versions from Homer / John Haffenden – William Empson in Japan / William Boyd – The Eleven Year War / Peter Morris – The Age of Consent / Simon Armitage – three poems

Issue 7 Bella Freud – The Art of Fashion / David Hare – The Art of Lying / Philip Gosse – Cancer: A Memoir / Matthew Leeming in Afghanistan / Sex, drugs & alcohol in Iran

Issue 8 Julian Barnes on syphilis / Patrick Marber's *Late One Night* / new fiction by Panos Karnezis / An interview with Enno Patalas

Issue 9 Ian McEwan on Love and Death / Ben Rice's first film script / August Kleinzahler on Ginsberg / new fiction by Philippa Stockley

Issue 10 Fiction by Adam Thirlwell / Interviews with Orhan Pamuk and Pawel Pawlikowski / A masterpiece by Dorothy Nimmo / Frederic Raphael on Stanley Kubrick

Issue 11 Tom Stoppard's unpublished screenplay – *Galileo*

Issue 12 Kipling's unpublished motoring diaries / Pasternak's unpublished suicide letter / Matthew Norman is stabbed in South Africa / Adam Thirlwell on Sebald / Craig Raine on Lowell

Issue 13 Unpublished poems by Vladimir Nabokov / Pleas and Directions – a play by Patrick Malahide / Interview with Christopher Logue

Issue 14 Evelyn Waugh on Hollywood / A radio play by Patrick Marber / William Boyd – a story / Harold Pinter on *Waiting for Godot*

Issue 15 Ian McEwan interviews John Updike / Peter Nichols's Diaries / Ann Pasternak Slater: The Case of Rudolf Kasztner / The genius of Richard van den Dool

Issue 16 William Golding – unpublished journals / Richard Eyre interviews Trevor Griffiths / Peter Nichols in New York / the reputations of Isaac Bashevis Singer, Philip Roth, Pablo Neruda, Marianne Moore

Issue 17 Longing – a play by William Boyd / interview with Mark Alexander / Fiction by Panos Karnezis and Julie Maxwell / reviews of Ishiguro, Akhmatova, Robert Lowell, Geoffrey Hill, Seamus Heaney, Christopher Logue

Issue 18 Homage to Joe Brainard: Patrick Marber, Ann Robinson, Sue Townsend, David Lodge, Wendy Cope, Harriet Walter, Dorothy Gallagher, Paul Farley, Josephine Hart, Ben Rice, David Mitchell, Michael Lesslie

Issue 19 Frances Stonor Saunders – The Woman Who Shot Mussolini / Veronica Horwell in Bosnia and the USA / Christopher Reid's great elegy / The Mother of a Murdered Prostitute: an interview

Issue 20 A Dialogue by Harold Pinter / Scenes from Ian McEwan's *Flies* / Phyllida Lloyd on Directing / Nicholas Murray on Sybille Bedford

Issue 21 Milan Kundera on the world of prose / Salman Rushdie, William Boyd, Adam Thirlwell, Alexander Nurnberg and Craig Raine on Kundera / interview with Celia Birtwell / Lucy Sisman on Design

Issue 22 Tom Stoppard in Moscow / fiction by Rose Tremain and Martin Krasney / Susan Hitch on being a film star / Craig Raine on Don Paterson / Adam Foulds's *The Broken Word* / Milan Kundera on horoscopes

Issue 23 Tom Stoppard's new radio play / Deaf Sentence – fiction by David Lodge / an interview with Francis Wyndham / a prose poem by Harold Pinter / T S Eliot as Publisher / Julian Barnes on doing grief / Craig Raine on Larkin the romantic

Issue 24 Robert Craft on Stravinsky: an interview / Steven Pinker and Ian McEwan in conversation about language / Why Margaret Atwood is a bad novelist

Issue 25 Evelyn Waugh: Unpublished Letters / poetry by Pinter, Reid, Groarke, Stead / John Barth: Introductions / Female Circumcision / Craig Raine on Elizabeth Bishop

Issue 26 Patrick Marber's screenplay *Love You More* / Stan Lauryssens: the Eichmann Diaries / a Tribute to Christopher Logue

Issue 27 Updike's last interview / Claire Lowdon on the Army / Blake Morrison on Heaney / Adam Thirlwell on Dufy / Julie Maxwell on García Marquez / David Bellos on Tintin / Lucy Sisman: Screening Out Filth

Issue 28 Harold Pinter: a Celebration by Tom Stoppard, Patrick Marber, Richard Eyre, Nina Raine, David Hare, Ronald Harwood, Peter Nichols, Marigold Johnson, Susanna Gross, Francis Wyndham, Nick Hern, Nigel Williams

Issue 29 John Updike: a Celebration by Martin Amis, Nicholson Baker, Adam Mars-Jones, Adam Thirlwell, Louis Menand, Mark Lawson, Nicholas Wroe, Julie Maxwell, Craig Raine / The Reputations of Raymond Carver, John Cheever, William Golding, Roberto Bolaño

Issue 30 New fiction from Ian McEwan / Alan Bennett: an interview and a celebration by Nicholas Hytner, Duncan Wu, Craig Raine, Bernard Richards /David Simon and *The Wire*: an interview by Mark Lawson / Christopher Hart on Zadie Smith's essays

Issue 31 Salinger: For and Against: Joan Acocella, Archie Bland, Craig Raine, Adam Thirlwell, Louis Menand, Julie Maxwell, Alexander Nurnberg, William Skidelsky, Oliver Reynolds / Blue Whale: a film: Nina Raine, Moses Raine / Claire Lowdon on Henry Moore / My First Pogrom: Leonid Pasternak

Issue 32 David Hare's unpublished screenplay – *Lee Miller*

Issue 33 Patrick Marber on Mike Nicols / William Boyd on directing / Adam Mars-Jones the film critic / J M Coetzee, Chinua Achebe, Nadine Gordimer reassessed / Bryan Forbes / Emma Loach / Seven poems by Wendy Cope

Issue 34 Ted Hughes: Unpublished Letters / Matthew Ira Swaye: New Fiction / Academe: Peter Conrad, Craig Raine, Alexander Nurnberg / Emma Shearn in Sudan

Issue 35 Christopher Hampton gets expelled from school / Interview with Tomi Ungerer / Nicholson Baker and David Foster Wallace reviewed / Moses Raine: Stevie, a film

Issue 36 Music: Von Karajan, Thomas Ades, Margaret Faultless, Atonement: A Libretto by Craig Raine / Christopher Reid: The Suit of Mistress Quickly / New Fiction by Matthew Ira Swaye

Issue 37 New York: Lucy Sisman, Sam Leith, Richard Eyre, Peter Conrad, David Hare, Matthew Ira Swaye, Tom Shone, Isaac Raine / Before Sunrise: a film: Moses Raine / Camilla Long on Susan Sontag

Issue 38 The Failure Issue: Hugh Grant, Zoë De Toledo, Wendy Cope, Lucy Ellmann, Christopher Hart, Lucy Sisman / *Appomattox*: Christopher Hampton's Libretto for Philip Glass / Reviews of Hilary Mantel, Robert MacFarlane, Marilynne Robinson and Peter Carey

Issue 39 The Memoir Issue: Budd Schulberg on Scott Fitzgerald, Prue Leith, Richard Eyre, Sophie Elmhirst on Jean-Dominique Bauby, Craig Raine on Salman Rushdie, Claire Lowdon on Dorothy Gallagher / An Interview with Tamsin Greig / Ann Pasternak Slater on *Maus* / Duncan Wu on Alice Munro

Issue 40: ***Areté: A Retrospective***

Issue 41: Fifty Great Moments of Theatre: Nicholas Hytner, Joe Penhall, Roger Michell, Sam Mendes, Philip Pullman, Richard Eyre, Henry Hitchings, Tom Stoppard, Susannah Clapp, Mark Haddon, Ronald Harwood, Alastair Macaulay, Patrick Malahide, Trevor Nunn, Christopher Hampton, Tamsin Greig, Alan Howard, John Lahr, Imogen Stubbs, Harriet Walter, David Edgar, April de Angelis, Ralph Fiennes, Ian Rickson / Christopher Hampton on Jocelyn Herbert / James Wood on Beckett

Issue 42: Jeremy Sam's Libretto for *Don Giovanni* / Three poems by Wendy Cope / My English Teacher: Ian McEwan, William Boyd, Wendy Cope, John Ashbery, Charlotte Mendelson, Jessie Burton, David Lodge, Matthew Francis, Jeffrey Eugenides, Mark Ravenhill, Rose Tremain, Nicholas Shakespeare, David Hare, Adam Thirlwell, Oliver Reynolds / New Fiction by May-Lan Tan

UK – £7.99 each, plus £1 p&p per copy. Europe – 16 Euros. USA/Australia/New Zealand – $18. *Retrospective*: £12 UK, 25 Euros Europe, $35 overseas. Also available as a Kindle ebook from Amazon.

Please make cheques payable to 'Areté Magazine', 8 New College Lane, Oxford, OX1 3BN, UK

Or: order online at www.aretemagazine.com

Subscriptions: £21 – one year/three issues. (Europe: 42 Euros. Overseas: $65 USD.) Libraries/Insitutions £30 (Europe: 54 Euros. Overseas: $85 USD). Cheques payable to 'Areté Magazine', 8 New College Lane, Oxford, OX1 3BN, UK

Culture seeks to do away with classes. The great men of culture have laboured to divest knowledge of all that was harsh, uncouth, difficult, abstract, professional, exclusive; to humanise it, to make it efficient outside the clique of the cultivated and learned.

Matthew Arnold: *Culture & Anarchy*

Printed by Berforts Information Press, Southfield Road, Eynsham, Oxford, OX29 4JB